SLAM-DUNK
SUCCESS

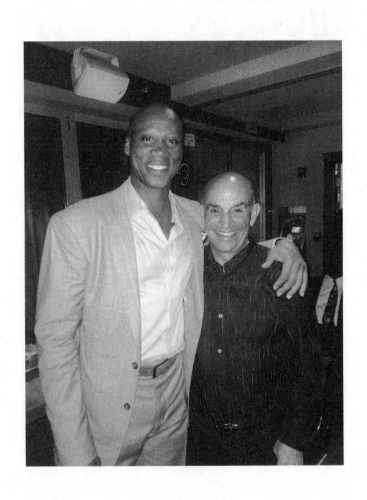

SLAM-DUNK SUCCESS

LEADING FROM EVERY POSITION ON LIFE'S COURT

BYRON SCOTT & CHARLES NORRIS

with **JON WARECH**

CENTER
STREET

New York Nashville

Center Street
Hachette Book Group
1290 Avenue of the Americas, New York, NY 10104
centerstreet.com
twitter.com/centerstreet

First Edition: April 2017

Center Street is a division of Hachette Book Group, Inc. The Center Street name and logo are trademarks of Hachette Book Group, Inc.

The publisher is not responsible for websites (or their content) that are not owned by the publisher.

The Hachette Speakers Bureau provides a wide range of authors for speaking events. To find out more, go to www.HachetteSpeakersBureau.com or call (866) 376-6591.

Library of Congress Cataloging-in-Publication Data has been applied for.

LCCN: 2017931929

ISBN: 978-1-4789-2044-1 (hardcover), 978-1-4789-2046-5 (ebook)

Printed in the United States of America

LSC-C

10 9 8 7 6 5 4 3 2

Contents

Foreword by Earvin "Magic" Johnson

Leadership is a funny thing. Most people think that you work your way up to becoming a leader. You win an NCAA championship, you get taken with the first pick of the 1979 NBA draft, you win a championship and are named the Finals MVP, and then you are the leader of the Los Angeles Lakers. But a true leader knows it's the other way around; you're a leader first and then you win.

It's not true just in basketball, but in every aspect of your life. If you're a college intern working in the business world for the first time, then that is your chance to shine. That's your opportunity to be a leader. Entry-level employee? Middle manager? Every department is looking for leaders, and those who take on that role are the successful ones.

Leaders are everywhere, leading by example, directly coaching others, motivating people around them, and helping their peers or even their superiors become better at what they do. On the Showtime Lakers I was a leader. I wasn't THE leader. There were a number of us, including Byron Scott, who spoke his mind, pushed us to be great, and played his heart out. When we needed him to be our leading scorer, he was our leading scorer. When we needed him to be a facilitator, he was a facilitator. That's leadership, and that's why we are five-time NBA champions.

Leadership is innate. You don't just leave it out there on the basketball court or in the locker room. When I retired from the game, I wasn't just going to retire from leadership. I had to shift my focus and be a leader elsewhere. Leaders are constantly changing the world around them, and they're doing it in a number of ways. There were business ventures—some good, some bad—and work to be done in my community. Sometimes I led financially, while other times I went in and made a difference with my own two hands. It's the reason I consider myself a success today. It's the reason I can look at not only my championship rings but also my portfolio of businesses and my reputation in the community and know that I'm a champion.

I went out and made victory happen, and you can too. I'll tell you one thing, though: I wish that when I was getting started in my career, I had a book like this. Byron and Charlie's detailed look into their overlapping business and basketball lives is the leader's handbook. By learning from their experiences, readers can see firsthand how to improve their own lives and nurture the necessary skills to be a champion in their chosen profession. These lessons are universal, and the best part is, anyone can do it.

Part of leadership is foresight, and I for one can tell you that I saw this book coming a mile away. I work out at Equinox with Charlie and Byron, and while most people did a double take when they saw those two working out together, I knew. Sure, they look different, and they come from different backgrounds, but mentally they're the same person. When those two would be laughing or sweating out sets on one of the machines, I knew it was also a meeting of the minds. I knew that while they had their differences on the surface, when it came to not only their goals in life but also how they went about achieving them, they were one and the same. Two competitive, intelligent, driven men like Charlie and Byron will always find each other, and thankfully they have joined forces to tell you their story.

As you read this book, think of your role on the team—think of where you are versus where you want to be—and know that from any position you can make a difference. You can be the leader. You can be the CEO of your life. You can be the Charlie Norris. You can be the Byron Scott. You can be the Magic Johnson. You can strive for greatness and walk away a champion. If picking up this book is the first step in empowering your leadership qualities, then the winning begins right now.

—Earvin "Magic" Johnson

Introduction

"Business is the ultimate sport." —*Mark Cuban*

Whether you are a basketball star in the NBA or a boardroom star with an MBA, the model for success is exactly the same. Follow the path set by Byron Scott and Charlie Norris and become the leader you always knew you could be.

BYRON SCOTT

I love basketball. I was out on the court shooting every day from the time I was physically able to pick up a ball. When I was twelve years old my dad asked me what I wanted to do when I grew up, and I immediately said I wanted to be a professional basketball player.

"That's great, that's great," he said. "But what if you don't make it?"

"I'm going to make it."

He laughed in my face. My mom was standing right there and started yelling at me about school.

"Oh, but you gotta keep going to school, you gotta get your education, you gotta, you gotta, you gotta…"

There were a lot of *you gotta*s before I could turn pro, and I heard all that, but as a twelve-year-old the only thing I could focus on was that *I gotta* be great.

From that day on, I worked every day and did everything I could to become the best basketball player that I could be. I practiced hard and I loved it. I pushed myself to be the best version of me both on and off the court. I gave everything to basketball.

Through high school in Los Angeles and college at Arizona State University, all I thought about was the NBA. "You got a chance" was what everyone would tell me. I started believing it. If there was a party that got in the way of what I was trying to achieve, then I wouldn't go. I wouldn't drink. I wouldn't smoke. I was determined and focused, and nothing was going to stand in my way. It was hard work, but when I finally did make it to the NBA, I realized that that was just the beginning.

CHARLIE NORRIS

I never had a long-term plan as a kid to become a CEO. Even in college at the University of Rochester I majored first in psychology and then in history. Business really crept into my mind as a career direction only when I was in graduate school at Northeastern University. I wasn't even sure I wanted to get an MBA, but I'm glad I did.

My whole life, though, I was interested in people. Even as a kid I wanted to know everything about the people around me, and I wanted them to know I was a hard worker. When I was shoveling snow, I made sure everyone in the neighborhood thought of me as the kid who would shovel snow.

As a teenager I bagged groceries, and I always talked to the customers. I found their lives fascinating, and in the back of my mind I always felt that they would think about me if there were other job opportunities in the community. I was driven by the thought of moving from bagging groceries to running the register, because

I always wanted to try something different. I always wanted more responsibility.

My dad worked very hard and he worked very intelligently. I saw that and became a person who just enjoyed hitting a goal. I did whatever it took to get there.

In a co-op program at Northeastern I realized how I could apply what I was learning in school to the workplace. It made me realize that the business world didn't stop at the checkout line. There was room to grow from salesman to manager and CEO. The sky was the limit, and I wanted to shoot for the stars. I liked working hard. There was a satisfaction to that. I wanted to be the best at whatever it was I was doing, and if that led me to being a CEO, then I would find a way to be the best at that.

BYRON SCOTT

In fourteen seasons in the NBA, I won three championships playing alongside the great Magic Johnson, Kareem Abdul-Jabbar, James Worthy, and the Showtime Lakers—a nickname we earned from our fast-paced, flashy style of play. Day in and day out Coach Pat Riley pushed me to be my best, and in every season my best was needed in different ways. In one of those years I was the team's leading scorer. In other years I was called on to be more of a defensive specialist. When I returned to the Lakers for one final season, I was more of a coach on the court, as young players like Kobe Bryant and Shaquille O'Neal were now the stars of the show.

Being a leader not only means doing whatever it takes to win, it also means making everyone around you better. Winning a championship takes all fifteen guys playing their best basketball. When I transitioned to coaching I focused on whatever was needed to turn each of those fifteen guys into the best version of themselves.

When I was a coach with the New Jersey Nets, we went to the NBA Finals twice. In New Orleans I won Coach of the Year with Chris Paul and the Hornets as we turned a once-mediocre team into a top contender in the Western Conference. In both cases I helped to mold young stars, squeezed a little extra out of aging veterans, and learned what made each player tick. It led to a lot of winning.

There were mistakes along the way. At times I was too tough. At times I was too stubborn. Other times maybe I was a bit too trusting. It led to losing—in small doses in New Jersey and New Orleans, and larger ones in Cleveland and Los Angeles.

Through it all I learned a lot about myself, including what it takes to be a leader in nearly any circumstance and how to push the right buttons to find greatness in every player. Mostly, though, I learned that I'd never stop learning.

CHARLIE NORRIS

I climbed the ranks as an executive, starting with the Scott Paper Company, where I worked as a sales rep while I was still in school. There I saw the value in marketing, but I also learned how to form business relationships. Negotiating by way of understanding people's wants and needs was a skill that I would use for the rest of my life.

I knew the only way to expand my horizons and meet all types of people was to explore the world. I took a job as a marketing manager at Rank Hovis McDougall in the UK and then became a project leader for Nestlé, a job that took me around the globe. I learned how different cultures interacted, conducted business everywhere from local markets to corporate headquarters, and put my foot in my mouth a number of times.

Growing as a leader means screwing up and learning from your mistakes. I did plenty of that, and by the time I was president of Deer Park Spring Water I had a better grasp of how to motivate people to strive for greatness.

There were a lot of great business wins over the years. I bought Deer Park for $3.5 million and sold it for over $20 million in twenty months. At McKesson Water we went from $220 million to over $400 million in sales, and sold the water division to Danone for $1.1 billion ten years later. Twenty months after partnering with a private equity firm to pay $12 million for Day Runner, we sold it for $45 million.

There were also failures and missteps, but the lessons learned from the good and the bad all led me to Freshpet, where I'm now chairman of the board of a company that I truly believe will reshape the pet food industry. The opportunity to be chairman of a publicly traded company was a new one for me, and even at my age, I'm still learning.

BYRON SCOTT

When I go to the gym, I'm there to exercise. It's been part of my routine nearly my whole life. Staying in shape is important to me not only on a personal level but also as a coach. I want to be on the court with the guys so they know I'm one of them—an older version, but one of them nonetheless.

At the Lakers' facility I talked to everyone. I enjoyed it and I learned from them. Most importantly, they are all part of the team, and each Lakers employee plays a role in the team's success. At

Equinox I'm on my own time, but as a leader I feel I should always be trying to better myself. Working out is part of that, but being part of the community, meeting new people, and creating new partnerships are also key to growing as a leader.

When I was introduced to Charlie, I liked him right away, but I had no idea where the friendship would go. He wanted to work out and valued his time at the gym in the same way that I did mine. When we starting working out together I saw how competitive he was—a characteristic I see all the time now when we play backgammon and boules (the French form of bocce) and even have the occasional shooting contest.

The friendship could have stopped there. That's what happens with most people. There's the surface-level friendship that develops where you become gym buddies or guys who go drinking together or whatever the case may be. What is important for all relationships (and what we want you to learn in this book) is that when you take relationships to a deeper level, you find more opportunities below the surface.

Charlie and I don't look alike, we don't have similar backgrounds, we're not even close in age, but we think almost exactly alike. He's my brother from another mother, and when I tell people about us they don't get it. But when they see us, they can feel our vibe. He's made me a better coach, a better businessman, and an all-around better person.

CHARLIE NORRIS

I feel the same way about my relationship with Byron. He made me better at my job by allowing me to observe how he does his job and by talking with me about both life and work situations. He's also made me a better backgammon and cards player—or at least I feel as if I'm better when I win.

When I met Byron, I was intrigued. Having grown up in Boston, I had been a Lakers hater all my life, but he was such a presence in the gym. Being a hometown hero and a person of his stature, Byron was a guy everyone at Equinox wanted to know. When I saw his ability to smile, shake hands, and have everyone in the room like him without its interrupting his workout, I knew he possessed qualities that I admired.

I didn't know what to expect when we first met. I had no idea what would come from it. I didn't even know if he really liked me or not. But once we started talking, we saw that despite our differences, we share a similar set of values and rules for success.

I noticed early on how cerebral Byron is. He analyzes situations, thinks about everything he says before he says it, and always seems to have a plan for himself and for the team. As a team-first guy myself, I usually had similar plans, so I knew pretty early we were going to do great things together.

Now we still push each other at the gym and crack jokes at each other's expense while doing it, but we also talk business strategy and ways we can work together to better each other's career. Running a basketball team and sitting on the board of a publicly traded company, surprisingly, have many similarities. Once we discovered that our collective set of rules for success in life were ultimately universal, we realized our potential to grow as leaders together was endless.

BYRON SCOTT

There was a time in my last season with the Lakers that I decided to bench Julius Randle and D'Angelo Russell. They weren't playing well, and they needed to earn their minutes back. I got beaten up in the media and by some in management who thought I was too old school. I just wanted the guys to play better.

One day I was with Charlie, who sat in on practices and on film sessions, so he'd seen what I was dealing with. We were on the elliptical machines at Equinox, and I was talking to him about connecting with these young guys. I was trying to communicate with them and they just weren't getting it.

"I'm just trying to figure out a way that they can really get it," I said.

"Why don't you put it in question form to them?" he asked. "Ask them, 'What's blocking you from being great?' and see how they respond."

I just smiled. I liked where this was going, and because I knew Charlie so well I knew exactly what he was going to say next.

"After they answer," he said, "ask them, 'How can I help you get there?'"

So I went to each of those players and did just that. I gave them time to think about it too. Julius Randle's answer was phenomenal. He said he was blocking himself and pointed out the mistakes he was making. Then, when I asked how I could help, he said, "Coach, hold me accountable." I jumped up and gave him a big hug.

But all the young guys took to the exercise, and it helped them grow. It opened their minds up to thinking about what they need to do to be successful, and it will stay with them their entire careers. Five years from now, if they are struggling at some point in their season, they'll ask themselves, "What's blocking me?"

I was looking for a new way to connect with them and for a new perspective on it, so I went to Charlie, who helped me get to the hearts and minds of these kids. If that's old school, then I'm old school and I'm proud of it.

Charlie and I have similar leadership models. His work in the business world isn't about short-term victories; it's focused on long-term championships. One or two bad financial years to ultimately turn a company into something worth ten times its original value is worth it, especially if the employees become better at what they do along the way.

It's what we do, and it's what you should do too. That's why this book is necessary. It brings together our two very different worlds and shows that the concepts behind solid leadership are the same in any arena. Life isn't about small victories, it's about figuring out what's blocking you from greatness and finding a way to be a champion. This book is our way of asking, "How can we help?"

CHARLIE NORRIS

Byron has truly always cared about his players and wanted them to be successful. He knows which of them can handle his really getting on them, and which need a hug sometimes. He puts them first and thinks about their long-term success and how it helps the team.

Leadership isn't about what's best for right now. It's not even about what's best for the leader. It's about doing the right thing for the team and making sure the future remains bright for everyone involved. That's what has made Byron a success.

That winning mentality has translated to success off the court as well. Just as with the players, Byron has a way with business leaders. He'll come with me to meetings and wow investors with his charm and knowledge of our industry.

He's a huge asset to have in business, and it's worked in both our favors, as he's invested in a number of the projects I'm working on. Yes, we have fun going to dinners, traveling, and playing all sorts of games for high stakes—sometimes as much as five dollars changes hands at a time—but at my age it's nice to have a new person around who helps me to be a better leader as well.

This book isn't about making new friends. We are using the foundation of our friendship to show you how two people from different worlds can have the same leadership qualities. If you want to be an NBA champion, an all-star in the boardroom, or anything in between, you will likely live by these same core values. Our joint knowledge proves that no matter what your profession, the ball is always in your court when it comes to leadership.

There will always be an obstacle between you and success, whether it's the need to motivate others, negotiate, build a winning organization, or improve your own personal leadership skills, but there's always a path to victory. Even in failure there is victory, and both Byron and I have experienced that and later found success because of it.

Leadership is a 24-7 quality. You should never turn it off. To be an effective leader you have to be an effective listener, treat people with respect, and find learning opportunities within every experience at the workplace and everywhere else life takes you.

As you read this book about what was blocking us and how we dealt with it, think about what's blocking you. Hop on the metaphorical elliptical with us, and let's figure it out together.

Timeline

CHARLIE NORRIS

Marketing manager, Rank Hovis McDougall, UK	1971–1972
Project leader, Nestlé S. A., Switzerland	1973–1976
Director of new ventures, Nestlé USA	1977–1980
President, Deer Park Spring Water Co.	1981–1990
President, McKesson Water Products Co.	1990–2000
Senior vice president, McKesson Co.	1993–2000
Chairman and director, Glacier Water Services Inc.	2001–2016
Chairman and director, Day Runner Inc.	2003–2004
Chairman and director, Freshpet Inc.	2006–present
Director, Manna Pro Products Llc.	2015–present
Director, Primo Water Corp.	2015–present

BYRON SCOTT

Playing:

Los Angeles Lakers	1983–1993
Indiana Pacers	1993–1995

Vancouver Grizzlies	1995–1996
Los Angeles Lakers	1996–1997
Panathinaikos, Greece	1997–1998

Coaching:

Sacramento Kings (assistant)	1998–2000
New Jersey Nets	2000–2004
New Orleans Hornets	2004–2009
Cleveland Cavaliers	2010–2013
Los Angeles Lakers	2014–2016

SLAM-DUNK
SUCCESS

Chapter 1

Honesty at the Top

"Whoever is careless with truth in small matters cannot be trusted in important affairs." —Albert Einstein

Being the boss is a tricky business, but the secret to success lies in how you treat people. Whether it's someone's first day on the job or their last, honesty goes a long way, especially when you realize how small the world is in your particular field.

BYRON: SURPRISE ENDINGS

The opportunity to be the head coach of the Los Angeles Lakers was a dream come true. When I got the call telling me it was even a possibility, all these emotions ran through my head. I'd played eleven seasons with the Lakers, six times going to the NBA Finals and three times winning a championship. I grew up in Los Angeles, fourteen blocks from the Forum. This was my team, and this was the job of a lifetime.

Jim Buss, the part owner and executive vice president of the organization, and General Manager Mitch Kupchak brought me in for several interviews and began the talks by saying one thing:

"The first two years are going to be really tough, are you OK with that?"

My response was, "I am OK, but are *you* OK with that?"

I could handle it. I knew what I was signing up for—a team with a lot of young players, an aging Kobe Bryant in the final years of his career, and an organization that was building for the future. A championship was out of the question from day one, but I knew winning basketball in LA, and I was confident I could bring us to that level once we had the right pieces in place.

I signed a two-year deal with a team option for a third year, but the talk was always that I would re-sign. We all agreed this was a three- or four-year project. They knew it. I knew it. We all knew what those first years were going to be like, and I trusted them when they said I was part of their long-term plans.

That was my thought process through the negotiations—they know me, I know them, I can trust them. When you tell me something and look me in the eye as you say it, I take it as gospel, because that's how I am. I'm honest, and I expect honesty. Especially with people like Mitch and Jim, whom I'd had a relationship with for years; I expected them to stay true to their word.

That's what hurt the most when Mitch broke the news after just two seasons that they were going in a different direction. I felt deceived. I felt that Jim Buss and Mitch Kupchak had used me to get through those final two years of Kobe Bryant's career and saved their own butts by making me the scapegoat. It seemed as if that had been their plan all along. I may bleed purple and gold, but after that meeting, the blood was all over management's hands.

I talked to a number of people in the following days. Jerry West.

Kobe Bryant. Longtime Lakers trainer Gary Vitti. They all showed their support, as well as their shock at the team's decision.

My dad called me the next day to see if I was OK. I said, "Pops, I'm good." Then he called my girlfriend Cece.

"Cece, this is your soon-to-be-one-of-these-days father-in-law," he said. (Of course she wanted me to know that part.) "I know my son, and he has a tendency to hold a lot of things in, so look after him. He won't let you know if he's really hurting, so just take care of him for me."

He knows because he's the same way. Where I grew up it was considered a sign of weakness for a man to show his emotions. As I've gotten older and had kids of my own, I've tried to let that go. I think it's important to let your kids see you laugh and cry. But in situations like this it's tough. I don't cry over spilled milk.

I went home, decompressed, and went to the gym the next morning. Mentally I had moved on. There was nothing I could do about it, so I wasn't going to dwell on it.

CHARLIE: THE COMPANY OVERHAUL

After years of working in the packaged food and bottled water industry for Nestlé, and buying and selling Deer Park, I was hired as president of McKesson Water Products Company. It was a large company that did $220 million in sales, and I had 2,500 employees working under me, so this was a big opportunity and a challenge I was ready to accept.

My predecessor, who had been promoted to a senior management position at McKesson Corporate—the parent company of McKesson Water Products Company—had made only modest changes to the company. The profit was going up by 5 percent annually because

McKesson Water raised the prices each year, but it wasn't growing as a company. We didn't have a platform from which to grow.

There was no centralization. No system in place. McKesson Water had three different water brands—Sparkletts, Alhambra, and Crystal—and when it purchased a new company, that company would have to create a new strategic business unit with its own general manager, marketing team, and accounting department. Financially and operationally, it didn't make much sense.

Our share was declining, and the customer quit rate was huge. Money from the price increase was being spent on recreating the old seltzer bottle and developing a line of fruit-flavored sparkling water instead of on helping to improve the trucks, the uniforms, and the efficiency of the routes, so route drivers were beside themselves. No one was listening to them, so they started an organizing drive. Rome was burning and nobody even knew it.

That's what I walked into, and I knew right away that for some time I was likely going to be the bad guy.

I knew what I needed to do. I knew a lot of people would have to lose their jobs. It was heartbreaking for me to disrupt the lives of so many people, but if I didn't do it the company would be out of business, and all 2,500 people would be back on the job market.

To pull this off the right way, I first needed to gain credibility, so I brought in an outside consulting firm so the managers I'd inherited could see what the 2,500 employees thought about the business—including the 230 in finance and administration, which is ridiculously high for a $220 million business.

Sparkletts was a family business that McKesson Co. had bought. Nobody ever got fired. If someone wasn't capable, Sparkletts found a job for him or her somewhere else in the company. It had terrible technology. Closing the books took three weeks at the end of the month. It was a mess. There was no central control. If I wanted to bring in a new advertising agency I had to get the marketing managers from all the strategic business units to agree on it.

I needed to consolidate, and the consulting firm proved that, but I still had to create the logic trail to show why restructuring and letting a lot of people go made sense. I think the firing process should be almost as thorough as the hiring process. It just seems like the right thing.

Linda Rush, the head of human resources, was my psychiatrist during all of this. She had been with the company a long time, through different management systems, and she understood we needed to centralize everything. She listened to me vent daily about our lack of systems, but more importantly, she was on board with my vision for the company. There were mornings when I thought I was going to lose my mind and evenings where a few drinks were definitely in order, and she was right there for it all, keeping me sane and providing necessary feedback to keep me on the right path.

It took nine months to build up enough of a story to explain to the organization why we needed to centralize operations. I knew we could do it quick and ugly, or we could take forever, and if we took forever it might not be ugly, but it wouldn't be effective.

I went to the CFO of McKesson Co. to tell him my plan, and he said that if I kept raising prices like my predecessors I would get promoted like everyone else, or I could do it my way and probably lose my job. He further said that I could do this, that it was what needed to be done, but that I would undoubtedly lose my job in the process and the person who succeeded me would benefit.

But it wasn't about me. I had been hired for a job, and in my mind the only option was to save this company. Unfortunately, for that to happen, a thousand people needed to go.

BYRON: BUSINESS OVER BASKETBALL

When you've been in this league as long as I have, you've seen a lot when it comes to relationships and how people handle things. When I was the head coach of the then–New Orleans Hornets, the owner at the time, George Shinn, was telling the coaches and the players and the whole city, really, that he and General Manager Jeff Bower were going to do whatever it took to bring a championship to New Orleans. Money was no issue, he said…until, of course, it was an issue.

Behind closed doors Mr. Shinn told Bower that he wasn't willing to pay a luxury tax, so he needed to trade whoever it took to get under the tax line. First on the chopping block was Tyson Chandler.

I was on the team bus when I got the news that TC had been traded to Oklahoma City, and I was not happy about it. Bower tried to convince me that we didn't need him, but not only was he a great player, he was a great locker room guy. Everyone on the team loved him, and that team had great chemistry on and off the court.

To me Tyson was invaluable to our team. He was the most positive guy I had been around as a coach. He always came to practice with a smile, worked, never complained, kept his teammates in check, and, most importantly, was our best defensive communicator. He did all the little intangible things that don't show up on the stat sheet but that a team needs to do to be championship caliber.

So I was sitting on the bus and David West walked on and he just stared at me for like three minutes. "I know how you're feeling," I said. "I'm feeling the same way too, but this is not my doing."

He just shook his head and headed to the back of the bus. When we got to the arena, the locker room was as quiet as I've ever heard it. It was like a funeral. Everybody was sitting in there with heads down.

I tried to encourage them. "I'm very disappointed too," I said. "I did not want this done, but life goes on, and we have to still play basketball. Our job is to come out here tonight and win a ball game. We have to put all this behind us for a while and go out there and focus on the game at hand."

Like true professionals, they went out and won. But they were angry at the owner, and they expressed that in the media afterward.

A day later the trade was rescinded. Tyson failed a physical with Oklahoma City and was sent back to our team. It was crazy. We had a gala event with the organization shortly after, and both Tyson and Mr. Shinn were there with their wives.

"Can you talk to him?" Shinn asked me about Tyson. "You know I'm trying to talk to him. He won't talk to me. He won't return my calls."

Tyson wouldn't give him the time of day. He was angry and rightfully so, but I tried.

"Screw him. I'm not calling him. I want nothing to do with him," was TC's response.

Then their wives got into it a bit, with Mr. Shinn's wife telling Tyson's wife what Tyson should be doing, which Tyson's wife did not take kindly to. It was an awkward scene, the kind of thing that can happen when you don't handle these situations properly.

If you sit in your ivory tower and move parts around as if they are not human beings, the players are not going to appreciate that. Then when the deal falls through and you want to be a guy's buddy again, it's not going to happen. Had Mr. Shinn handled it differently, he and Tyson might have been able to work things out. Overall it was just bad business, which is ironic from someone who had thought he was making a "business decision."

CHARLIE: ACCEPTING CHANGE

We went from 2,500 to 1,500 employees. It was a hard decision to make because I value loyalty, and in my first year on the job I was forced to break trust with a significant number of the employees. In order to let the team know that I had their best interests at heart, and that they should hold on to their trust, I didn't just jump in and hand out pink slips across the board. I created task forces of frontline employees who made recommendations about what departments and jobs should be eliminated. They knew even better than senior management how inefficiently the company was run. Some employees even recommended the elimination of their own positions. Even though the task forces were on board, it was still hard for me to watch so many hardworking people pack up their boxes.

Every case was different, of course, and many times when I thought a person could be well suited to another position I tried to make that shift happen. Even as the company moved forward, I wanted to reward the loyalty of those who had stood by this decision.

One guy, we'll call him Jim, had an MBA from a prestigious university and was an expert on strategic planning. His background was more staff than line, so I brought in somebody else as VP of marketing, even though that's the job that Jim wanted. I didn't think that he'd be well suited for it.

We had a small division called Aqua Vend, the precursor to Glacier Water. The person who had been running Aqua Vend was a longtime Sparkletts guy who was past his prime. Seeing the changes that were forthcoming, he decided to retire. I thought this was an opportunity for Jim to really see if he could run something.

I put him in as the general manager of Aqua Vend, and it was not a good fit. He was not an operating guy. He was overthinking things and doing far more analysis than necessary. He was getting caught in analysis paralysis, and not getting to answers. He had these lengthy presentations, but the Aqua Vend division never hit its numbers. So finally I said we had to make a change.

Since he had been so loyal to me, I wanted to do it in the softest way possible—a way that gave him the greatest flexibility to find another job and do it well. I called him into my office and I said, "Jim, we've got to make a change. You're going to have to leave the company, but I want you to think about it, and come back to me with how you want to do this. We can give you severance. We can announce this however you'd like. Think about it, come back to me in a couple of weeks, and tell me what you want to do."

A couple of weeks went by and I didn't hear from him, so again I set up a meeting.

"Jim," I said. "You were going to come back to me in a couple of weeks."

"Oh, yeah," he said. "I'm busy with the business and I have all these great ideas for what should happen with the business."

"No, Jim, you're not getting it. I want you to tell me how you would like the announcement to go on how you're leaving. That's all you need to be doing."

A couple more weeks went by, and this time I had Linda in the room when he walked into what was now our third meeting.

"I figured out the right organization for Aqua Vend, and I need to fire this person and that person, and then we'll have a smoother organization for me to operate from."

"Jim, you're not getting it," I said. "You're just not understanding.

I'm talking about you leaving. Come back to me next week, and this time you'd better have something."

He came in and again he started talking about changes, but I'd had Linda have an outplacement person waiting outside. This time I said, "Jim, you're done as of today. The outplacement person will escort you and set you up for outplacement services."

We needed to escort him out of the building. We arranged to send his personal belongings to him. He was gone. That's just the way it works sometimes. Even when you try to do things the right way and allow the employee to exit on his own terms and start a new life elsewhere, it doesn't go well. As a leader you don't want a situation like this to discourage you and break your spirit for the next time, but sometimes you just have to fire someone and move on.

BYRON: PARTING WAYS PROFESSIONALLY

This wasn't the first time the Lakers had let me go. After I'd played for them for ten seasons and won three championships, my contract was up and I was told they weren't going to re-sign me.

Jerry West, the general manager at the time and a mentor to me throughout my career, called me into his office to tell me man-to-man.

His eyes started to tear up. He was the one who'd brought me to the Lakers, and we had been through so much together that this moment was just emotional for both of us.

"Listen," he said. "We've got to move forward. There's this kid Anthony Peeler. We're going to go with him. You've been great in this organization."

"Jerry, I just appreciate it," I said with tears in my eyes. "Thank you so much for everything."

At that point, being a Los Angeles Laker was all I had ever known. Having played alongside Magic Johnson, Kareem Abdul-Jabbar, James Worthy, and all my great teammates over the years, including even Mitch Kupchak, I felt I was part of something special. Nearly every season we were championship contenders, and we played a style of basketball that changed the game and left a mark on the history of the NBA.

When I walked out of Jerry's office, I was sad it was over, but in my heart I was happy I had gotten to be part of that run.

Afterward reporter Jim Hill came over to my house and asked me a few questions on camera, and I just told him the same thing. I said that I loved the organization and had no hard feelings for Jerry West, owner Dr. Buss, or anyone with the Lakers.

I knew I was leaving, but that in my heart I would always be a Laker. That's why it was so important for me to leave on good terms. I took pride in wearing the purple and gold, and to me the team was like family. Business is business, so in sports there always comes a time when you have to part ways, but when you get to shake hands with and even hug the general manager on your way out, you know you handled business the right way.

Three years later I returned to the Lakers and played my final season in the NBA for the team I loved. And eighteen years after that, I returned as head coach. That's what happens when you do business the right way. You can do a good job, leave, have other experiences, and return in a different capacity to a place you consider your home.

Along the way you never know when the guy who was sitting

next to you in one job is going to be the guy hiring you for another. Every relationship is important, not just because of what the other person might do for you someday, but also because of how you can affect the other person's life. If you treat people with respect, you'll walk away a winner no matter the situation.

When you get treated like family, you can always return. When you're just an employee, none of that matters. This time around, as coach of the Lakers, I was disappointed in Mitch, but even though it ended on a sour note, my years of love for and loyalty to the Lakers make this a bond that can't be broken.

I don't hold anything against Mitch whatsoever. He's going to continue to be the GM and bring that team to championship-caliber basketball. Holding a grudge takes too much energy. It's not my style. And to be honest, it's bad for business. Dwelling on the past prevents you from making good decisions for your future. This experience with the Lakers was just another lesson learned. It was one that could test the heart of a champion but not one that could break it. I've come too far to let that happen.

CHARLIE: HELPING PEOPLE MOVE ON

It ended up taking four years to turn around the McKesson Water Products Company, much longer than expected, because the California economy tanked, but we centralized everything—one person running marketing, one person running routes, one person running manufacturing. We became very sophisticated. We had data on every customer, employees voted not to join a union, the route drivers were making more money, and we cut an annual 60 percent quit rate in half. We even increased the employee base back to 2,500, with our average sales per employee double what it had been the first time around.

We went from $220 million to over $400 million in sales. Six years after that we sold the water division to Danone for $1.1 billion. My top eight executives all became millionaires. It all worked out in the end, but getting there was tough, especially when it came to having to fire a thousand people.

People fear the unknown, so they have a hard time letting go. What I have found is that if you give honest feedback to people, they know if it's working or not working. Even though they are afraid of what the future can bring, more often than not it works out best for that person as well as for the organization. I've had a number of people thank me after the fact because being let go gave them a chance to step back and say, "What should I really be doing?" Even fairly senior people often end up in a much better place.

Jim was a very bright guy. He could have been a college professor. He could have been writing books. At his core he was really a staff person, someone who should have been working with an expense budget and not a profit-and-loss responsibility. He would have fit in well at a department that studies market research and tells the line people what customers are saying about the company's products. That's the kind of thing he was good at. He could have done that anywhere. There were lots of places where his skill set would have been more applicable.

At McKesson Water we hired outplacement specialists who did testing to find what other areas might be more appropriate for a person's skill set, helped with résumé building, and gave people an office so they weren't sitting at home and wondering what they should be doing. We helped as much as we could, and I think people appreciated that.

By the time I left, it's safe to say I was a pretty popular guy at McKesson Water, and I like to think it's because management treated people with respect and did things the right way. But we still had to say good-bye to people who were like family to many in the company. That takes a toll on a leader emotionally, and you spend a lot of time tossing and turning at night, thinking about the lives affected by the restructuring. But I had no choice. Without the complete overhaul, all 2,500 employees would have eventually lost their jobs. Nonetheless, it was one of the hardest things I've ever had to do.

X's and O's

- A lifelong relationship can be ruined in an instant if you don't treat people with the proper respect.

- You have to care for an employee on the way out in the same way you did when they were on the way in.

- After someone leaves a job, the relationship isn't necessarily over so treat a person as if you might work with him or her again.

- If you are honest and open about the decisions you make, people will trust and respect you even if that decision affects them negatively.

Chapter 2

Joining the Team

"The whole is greater than the sum of its parts." —Aristotle

In any aspect of life, being a team player is a necessary trait of a champion. Earning your stripes leads to acceptance, team unity, and ultimately a winning organization. The best time to become that team player, of course, is your first day on the job.

BYRON: CONFIDENCE FROM THE TOP

My rookie year got off to a rocky start, because I was drafted by the then–San Diego Clippers and traded before the season to the Los Angeles Lakers for Norm Nixon, who was a popular guy in LA. Everyone in the city was pissed off about it—the players, the fans, Jack Nicholson. Before they even saw me play one game I was disliked in my own hometown.

I was born in Utah, but I grew up in Inglewood, California—a neighborhood that was gang infested but also filled with a lot of good people who were often overlooked and underappreciated. Most of the guys who grew up on my street and the neighboring streets were athletes, so we'd play touch football in the streets or basketball at my friend's house nearly every day. It was rougher than most neighborhoods, but I knew early on that I wanted to play basketball, so I was able to stay focused and avoid trouble most of the time. My younger brother was always in trouble and getting into fights, so from time to time I'd have to throw down, but I spent more time hitting jump shots than hitting faces.

My team was the Los Angeles Lakers. They played only a few blocks from where I'd grown up. So getting traded to them right away was a dream come true. Finding out that no one else was thrilled about it was kind of a nightmare, but it motivated me to play my best and prove people wrong.

The night we finally got the deal done, and the contract was signed, the Lakers actually had a game, so I watched it in GM Jerry West's office.

"Listen, I'm getting all this crap about making this trade, that it was one of the worst trades I've ever made," he said. "I'm going to tell you something right now—in three to five years, these people are going to be kissing my butt, because then they're going to be saying it's one of the best trades I ever made."

It was great for me as a rookie to hear the GM have that confidence in me. As a leader he wanted to challenge me to live up to his expectations, but also let me know that he had my back. It made me think, *This man stuck his neck out for me, and I'm not going to let him down. I'm going to bust my butt every day. I'm going to make sure he's right.* It gave me added motivation to make sure I went out every single day and played as hard as I could, and to be the best ballplayer I could be.

CHARLIE: LEARNING ON THE JOB

In graduate school at Northeastern University, I was on a work-study program that was six months of school and three months of working, followed by three months of school and six months of working, and a final three months of school. In that time I got a job with the Scott Paper Company.

For the first three months I worked for someone whose area of responsibility was Cape Cod, and it was his job not only to sell the product to the stores but also to negotiate how and where the product was displayed. As a graduate student I was basically executing what that salesman had organized with the store managers. I would go in the back room for product and put it on the shelf and build the displays.

Cape Cod was interesting because the population expanded dramatically in the summertime. In the wintertime it was pretty empty, so a good time for a worker to leave was the fall, just before both sales and temperatures dropped.

True to form, the salesman did just that, and instead of replacing him, the regional manager handed me the reins. If you have somebody you can follow and observe interacting with people, then that's a real benefit, especially if they're good at what they do. Watching for a while before you're thrown into the fire has a lot of positives to it, but in this situation that wasn't an option.

"You're a smart guy, figure out how to do it and do it," the regional manager told me, and he asked me to meet certain targets—more displays, more facings, more stock in the back room—that the company had budgeted for that area of the country.

Back in those days, with the supermarket chains, you often had flexibility within a given store to put a display up on the corner of an aisle, called a wing display, or you might get a full end-aisle display. You could sometimes get a store manager to give you more facings for a product and reduce somebody else's facings if you had an appropriate argument based on sales movement or, as my manager pointed out, if you simply had a good relationship with the store manager.

"The job is really about cultivating relationships with the store manager," he said as he explained my responsibilities. "The first time you go in, he doesn't know who you are and you don't know who he is. Don't even attempt to sell anything. Introduce yourself, tell him your background, and explain to him that you're going to be running the region for the next three months. Find out what his needs are and how you can be helpful to him."

BYRON: EARNING RESPECT

After the game was over, they took me to the locker room and introduced me to my teammates. I went around the room, and when I went up to Magic Johnson, he was putting on his shirt and barely making eye contact with me.

"All right, nice to meet you," he said. "You ready?"

"Yes, I'm—"

"All right, all right. You'll be at practice tomorrow, right?"

"Yeah, so I—"

"See you tomorrow."

It wasn't the warmest welcome that I've ever received, but I understood where he was coming from. The only one on the team who talked to me at all that first week was James Worthy. It was only his second year, and we had been in the same graduating class in college, so he wasn't yet in the position to be giving me the cold shoulder.

Kareem Abdul-Jabbar was the patriarch. He was older and wiser, and it wasn't in his personality to try to mold me into a champion. He wasn't trying to give me a hard time, but he wasn't trying to be my buddy that first year either. When he talked to me it was to say, "Get me some water, rook."

"OK, Cap. Sure thing, Cap. Whatever you say, Cap." Those were the only appropriate responses to anything your captain asked of you. When you're a rookie you do it. Maybe it's a little demeaning. You start a job, making real money for the first time in your life, playing the game you love, and your teammate is talking to you only when he wants water. But then you stop and realize it's Kareem Abdul-Jabbar and you get the damn water.

CHARLIE: PRIDE IS FOR THE EXPERIENCED

That was the first time I really understood that negotiation has to be a two-way street. You need to know what the person wants and what their hot buttons are in order to get them to be interested in what you're trying to sell. Little by little I would go into these stores—probably once every two weeks—to make a sale and do aisle resets.

Sometimes I would be asked to reset products I wasn't even selling. They needed hands and feet to help them with the aisle if they were doing a major reorganization of the entire section. Sometimes they'd say, "Could you come in on Tuesday and help us, because we want to reset this whole aisle." It wasn't a hazing situation such as Byron was going through, and it wasn't a lack of respect; it was merely a request for a favor.

As a young professional you can read that the wrong way and make a wrong decision. In my first job out of school in the early 1970s I was working in the United Kingdom for Rank Hovis McDougall, commercializing a protein product intended to enhance the quality of diets in third-world countries. On one occasion I flew to Mexico with the chief scientist to give a presentation to a Mexican government-owned company called CONASUPO that controlled all the sugar plantations and bakeries at the time. At the end of the week, when we were ready to leave, the scientist realized he'd forgotten something in his room. He casually told me to run upstairs and get whatever it was that he'd left.

I turned to him and said, "I'm not your butler."

The guy never spoke to me for the rest of the time I was at the company, and he was somebody I had to work with a good amount. It was my first job out of graduate school, and he was the top guy, and that's what I said to him...the top guy.

He had spoken to me in a very dismissive way, and it just didn't sit well with me at all. But that was a rookie mistake on my part. I should have just done it. I was a young guy, just getting started, and he—whether on purpose or not—was testing me. It was a simple task that would have changed our relationship for the years to follow, but instead I was labeled as the young guy with the bad attitude. Sometimes you need to swallow your pride when you are just getting started and be a leader by showing you can take a little heat.

BYRON: HAZED AND CONFUSED

Magic and Michael Cooper—they brought the heat. During the first week of practice they tested me. During scrimmages, with

Coach Pat Riley nearly working us to death, Magic and Coop were being physical and really putting me through it to see how I was going to react. It's different from what players do to rookies nowadays. The guys on the Lakers last year made the rookies bring doughnuts to practice, and collect all the balls when practice was over, and things like that. The rookies also had to come to practice and the game with backpacks on and strollers with Cabbage Patch dolls in them. In Cleveland they filled Dion Waiters's car with popcorn. It's silly hazing and a rite of passage—these rookies do it because the players before them did it as rookies, and to be in this fraternity you've got to pass the test.

When I was a rookie, though, there was none of that. I got water for Kareem because the man wanted water. The veterans weren't interested in silly games. Rookies came in and the veterans would just push them around, play them hard and throw them a couple extra elbows. They wanted to see how well the new guys could handle physical play. In my case they were also genuinely mad that the Lakers had traded Norm, so the elbows were real. It wasn't fun and games.

It was a tough adjustment for me at first—everyone giving me either the cold shoulder or a sharp elbow. In college at Arizona State University I had been a star. People had loved me. It was a rude awakening and a huge blow to the ego to have to start from scratch and earn that respect and admiration all over again.

What really helped me was that I was at home. After practice I could go and talk to my childhood friends, who are still my friends today, and my family, and be like, "These dudes is tripping." They'd tell me I was going to be fine, and that the guys would eventually embrace me if I just kept doing my thing. It's great to have a mentor or someone up top with confidence in you, so I thought about Jerry

West's words often, but it's also nice to have support from friends and family when you are just getting started. That kind of encouragement is priceless.

CHARLIE: BARGAINING CHIPS

When I was at Scott Paper it was a different story. I didn't want to ruffle any feathers, and I hadn't yet developed any sort of ego. At that point in life I had done some work for a food broker and I had bagged groceries at a store, so I knew the industry a little bit, but I wasn't too good for any job—which ultimately is how you should feel throughout your career, no matter what level you are at. If it helps the team, it's always worth doing.

During my time on Cape Cod, I saw the benefits of being a team player. When I did the store manager a favor, he'd do me a favor in return. I could say, "Can you throw up five cases on the wing here? I need to get to a certain total sales volume at the end of a quarter," and he would do it.

Improving the relationship went beyond the store. While stocking the shelves, I'd get to know him as a person, and I could go to my manager and say, "I've gotten to know Frank very well, I bet he would love to go to a Red Sox game. If I can get two tickets for the Red Sox game I think I can get him to give me X, Y, and Z." Every region had money for discretionary spending. If I could use it in a certain way, I could significantly increase what we were doing in a given store or even sometimes in small chains. One Red Sox game could mean the difference between a successful season and an unsuccessful one.

BYRON: STANDING UP FOR YOURSELF

So I took the pushing and shoving for about a couple weeks, and then one practice I got an elbow from Coop and I snapped.

"All right, that's it, next time any of y'all throw an elbow at me there's going to be a fight."

Coop, with his little high voice, said, "Oh, it's like that?"

"Yeah, it's like that."

That was a turning point, and later Magic told me that they had been testing me to see if I had any heart. That's what they wanted to find out, and I guess I passed the test.

A few weeks later, on one of our road trips, Magic called me over.

"Baby B, what you doing tonight?"

"I have no plans, man. I don't know anybody in any of these cities that we're going to."

"Wanna go to the movies with me and Coop?"

"Yeah, sure."

I felt like a little kid, all happy that I was accepted. That was the start of the so-called Three Musketeers. After that we were like brothers, close as could be. We hung out on the road, hung out at home.

The bond carried over onto the court as well, and those elbows helped in game situations too. In actual games you get elbowed and pushed around by guys who aren't your friends. The second I put on that Lakers uniform I was an enemy of the Boston Celtics and guys like Danny Ainge. I couldn't stand him, and I'm sure he couldn't stand me.

One of the first times I played against him, he elbowed me, but I kept my composure. My experience in practice certainly helped with that. Once Magic and Coop had put me through the wringer, there was nothing I couldn't handle from a guy like Ainge.

But I've always had the mentality in basketball and in life that when someone knocks me down, I'm going to wait until they forget about it and then knock them down even harder. I think that comes from my mom. She was a fireball. I saw my mom get challenged by another woman after my sister got into a fight with her daughter, and my mom said, with switchblade out, "I'll cut you up, y'all." She was not a confrontational person, but if you stepped to her she would never back down. She'd get you—sometimes when you least expected it.

So when we met the Celtics again months later, Magic knew that Ainge had it out for me and gave me some advice on how to get him back. I was ready to bring out the switchblade on him, so I would take all the advice I could get.

"Next time you're going to the basket, he's going to be on your left side," he said. "As you shoot, bring that elbow right to his chin, and watch, they'll call a foul on him."

Sure enough, it happened exactly as he'd said. I ripped through the lane, Ainge was on my left, and I clocked him in the chin and made the shot. The referee blew the whistle and said, "Count the basket."

"I told you," Magic screamed. "That's what I'm talking about! Yeah!"

I think all the ups and downs are good for rookies. They help with team chemistry and camaraderie, and they make you appreciate being part of the team more. Every rookie who comes in is different. Some think they are already the best player in the NBA. Some go through training camp and are overwhelmed. All this hazing, if you want to call it that, takes the attention away from the grind, puts every rookie on the same page, and ultimately makes them all part of the team. Then, before you know it, you're best friends with Magic and Coop, and it's Danny Ainge getting the elbows.

CHARLIE: THE MIND OF A SALESPERSON

Anyone in management benefits from some time in the sales force, because on the front line you learn more about the people you are selling to and also the end consumer. When you're in the store, you're looking at your aisle, and you can talk to people about why they selected your product instead of Kimberly-Clark's or Proctor & Gamble's. You learn what the competition is doing to take facings away from you, and you're right at the front line trying to protect your space. It becomes a game in which you figure out how to outmaneuver your competition at the store level, where you're displaying and selling your product.

That experience sets you up for a lifetime of understanding how the game works, and when you're thrown right into the mix, you learn on the job. But you also need a leader you can go to and feel confident in asking dumb questions. You have to be secure enough in your own capability that you know it's OK, because asking dumb questions is always better than making big mistakes.

I went to my supervisor with a number of questions, but still there were growing pains. During that time I was probably too quick to want to sell something, even though I had been specifically told not to rush into a sale. I had only a three-month window, and I wanted to show that I could get it done. I spent a lot of time building relationships with the important people in each store and learning who the decision makers were in the paper aisle, and I wanted to leave making sure I'd made the most of those relationships.

But I didn't need to rush. After the time in Cape Cod, I worked for Scott Paper Company for six months at its head office in Philadelphia in the advertising and promotion department, where I was involved in analysis of the different promotional vehicles the company was using. I was trying to determine what was working and what wasn't working. Eventually Scott offered me a full-time job, but I decided to go to England instead, where all of a sudden I was too good to be someone's butler.

X's and O's

- Being a team player means sharing your opinion, but executing without hesitation.

- Acceptance is earned, not given.

- No matter what, remember you are on the team for a reason: because you can add value.

- Every relationship in life, whether business or personal, is a two-way street.

Chapter 3

The Art of Focus

"You can always find a distraction if you're looking for one."
—Tom Kite

Whether it's celebrating early or being distracted by the competition, success can be thrown off by one false move. The key is making sure you learn from your mistakes and walk away better for having had the experience.

BYRON: PREMATURE CELEBRATION

Right from my rookie year I was on a team that was built to win, with Magic, Kareem, Coop, and James Worthy. There were also guys like Bob McAdoo, Kurt Rambis, and Mitch Kupchak, who all had long NBA careers as players and then coaches or general managers. I was the second youngest guy on the team (Worthy had me beat by a month) and the lone rookie, so I had to act like a winner from day one. That came naturally to me, because I had been winning all my life, but never at this level and never in the purple and gold.

We finished the regular season 54–28 and were the number one seed in the Western Conference. We cruised to the NBA Finals, beating the then–Kansas City Kings, the Dallas Mavericks, and Phoenix Suns along the way.

When I walked into the locker room after closing out the Phoenix Suns in game six, I was happy as hell. We were going to the Finals, which seemed like a big deal. But when you're a Laker, getting to the Finals is not a cause for celebration. I looked around the locker room, and it was business as usual. Magic was the orchestrator of that. We looked to him, and when he wasn't celebrating, we knew we shouldn't be celebrating either. Nobody was saying anything, so I sat down and just chilled out for a minute, and then showered, dressed, and went back to Los Angeles.

In the 1990–91 season we beat the Portland Trail Blazers to go back to the Finals, and Sam Perkins, who had joined the team after six seasons in Dallas, came running into the locker room jumping around, ready to party. Everyone just kind of looked at him, and someone pulled him aside and said, "Sam, we don't celebrate winning the Western Conference here. We only celebrate championships."

It was funny because he apologized, and then we apologized to him. At that point we had forgotten what it was like to get there for the first time. There's no pleasure in second place, so we just never celebrated until there were rings on our fingers, but there should be some joy in the journey.

That's how it was my first year too. The day after winning the Western Conference Finals, we went to practice and started looking at video of Boston, and I was just like, *OK, I guess this is normal.*

That's the kind of focus we had as a team. We didn't have time for emotions.

CHARLIE: WORLDLY EXPERIENCES AND FOREIGN MISTAKES

A lot of young people now look at the opportunity to see the world as a bridge between completing their education and starting in their careers. When I was coming out of school, people didn't normally do that. Most people just went right to work, which I wanted to do, but I also wanted to expand my horizons.

Scott Paper Company was considered one of the best consumer packaged goods companies in the United States, and after graduate school, it offered me a job. I could have gotten a traditional packaged goods background, but I wanted to see the world. Part of that wanderlust may have come from my dad, who grew up in Poland, was a Zionist who wanted to end up in Palestine, went to the University of Algiers as an undergraduate to study winemaking, and then went to the University of Copenhagen for graduate school, where he studied both milk and cheese making and traveled quite extensively. He spoke seven languages and was truly a global person.

Consciously or not, I followed in his footsteps by working for Rank Hovis McDougall for two years in London and then for Nestlé, which was headquartered in Switzerland. I moved from a large Boston suburb to the giant city of London to a village of 1,200 people above the thriving metropolis of Vevey, where Nestlé's global headquarters were located—a city that was all of twenty thousand people in its own right. It was a big adjustment.

At Nestlé I was responsible for soy protein development on the culinary side globally. We could reconstitute soy in different forms and could make products that actually resembled chicken strips, beef chunks, and ground beef.

My job was to pick prime mover countries and work with local

Nestlé companies to determine what form of soy product we should be making, packaging, and selling there.

I had to learn the different culinary habits of each target country and figure out in what form my soy-based products would be best received, so I moved around from country to country developing these products. My first assignment brought me back to the UK, where I produced a successful ground beef soy product called Mince-Saver during a time in the seventies when beef prices had gone through the roof. It was named the third most successful product launch in the UK that year. It was my first launch, and we got it right.

To me that felt like a cause for celebration. Third best isn't *the* best but it's pretty great. I'd never experienced this level of success before and, much like Sam Perkins, I was pretty damn happy. So was the head of Nestlé in Japan, who wanted me to ride the wave of success and create a version of this product in Asia. So just like that I was off to Japan.

At that time every Japanese woman had to know how to make six or eight basic dishes in order to be considered eligible for marriage. Many of them went to cooking school, while those who couldn't afford it watched cooking programs on TV.

So I went to cooking schools to observe and worked with a market research firm founded by George Fields, who wrote many of the early books on how to do business in Japan. We were trying to bring a soy-based product to a country that was just moving out of soy-based products. They were proud of the fact that they were eating meat, and Kobe beef had become important, so selling them on putting soy back into their diets was not easy. What we had done easily in the UK was very difficult to translate to the culinary structure of Japan.

After rigorous research and working with George, we ended up developing ingredients that when added to ground beef made a Western-style hamburger. We used different spices that gave the meat and soy a certain Western flavor. We were downplaying the meat-extension angle and playing up that it was an old-fashioned American burger.

In the seventies Japanese businesses took a much longer time to evaluate an idea, but once they got it they moved much faster. We put this product in a test market and it did extremely well. Ajinomoto, which was much larger than Nestlé on the culinary side in Japan, saw what we were doing, copied it, and went national while we were still in a test market. Being number two wasn't going to be profitable behind a giant like Ajinomoto, even though we had developed the product and we were doing incredibly well in test. This for me was a punch in the gut, and it really riled me up.

You can never assume you are doing anything in isolation. You always have to assume that there will be a reaction from the competition. And in this case the competition got the best of us, which adversely affected my next decision.

BYRON: HEAD GAMES

Before the series started we felt we were the better team. They were tough, with Larry Bird, Robert Parish, Kevin McHale, Dennis Johnson, and Danny Ainge. They were fighters, but we felt our skills were better in every category.

We took game one on the road and game three at home to put us up 2–1 in the series. With game four at home, we felt we had a huge advantage. But the Celtics had different ideas. They knew they weren't going to outshoot us, so instead they decided to push us around. It started small, but escalated during a key play that would change the momentum of the series.

Kareem passed the ball halfway down the court to James Worthy, who sent it across to Kurt Rambis, who was set for an easy layup until Kevin McHale, who was running to catch up, came in and clotheslined him. Kurt hit the floor hard—headfirst—and his goggles went flying. It was nasty looking. He shot up to go after him, the benches cleared, and all hell broke loose. James tried to stop Kurt, but he wanted McHale's head.

Back then there were no ejections or suspensions or even technical fouls for this kind of thing. The referees got everyone back to the benches, and Kurt shot two free throws. It was just a regular foul, but because of it, they got in our heads.

We lost all focus after that. We became so angry as individuals that instead of just trying to win the game, each of us was focused on trying to take McHale out to get back at the Celtics. Kareem got into it with Larry Bird, and James had a thing with Cedric Maxwell. I remember just wanting to kill Danny Ainge and Gerald Henderson.

All of a sudden we weren't even thinking about basketball. But if you notice, after that first fight, Kurt ended up back on his butt for a second time and Bird actually helped him up off the floor. He wasn't doing it to be a nice guy. He was showing that he wasn't fazed. He didn't lose his cool. We were all in the same fight, but the Celtics won the chess match and eventually the game in overtime after we blew a lead.

We didn't talk about it after the game, but subconsciously I think each one of us had a new game plan moving forward: revenge. It was a bad plan. The Celtics always looked at us as tuxedo-wearing Hollywood boys and saw themselves as hard-hat East Coast tough guys. What was dirty to us was normal to them, so once they started a brawl, we were all of a sudden trying to play their game instead of focusing on Lakers basketball, which is getting up and down the court, executing on offense, and getting easy buckets.

Because of it, we lost the series in a game seven in Boston. The fans stormed the court in celebration and were pushing us and trying to rip our jerseys off. I walked to the locker room behind Kareem, who was just punching people left and right to clear a lane. He had his fist cocked and was just knocking people out.

Afterward I don't remember what Pat Riley said or what Magic said. I just remember taking a shower and just sitting by my locker in shock. We were better than they. I knew we were. Yet somehow we were left sitting in the locker room, listening to the partying going on outside the Boston Garden. Normally we spend about forty-five minutes in the locker room. That night we sat for about two hours before Riles said we had to go.

CHARLIE: FINDING VICTORY IN FAILURE

I moved on to Nigeria to test the expansion of our soy products in that region. As I had in Japan, I had to learn the culture of the country and not just what products the people appreciate, but why they appreciate them.

Nigeria is a country of storytelling, and a lot of it happens around the stew pot, which is cooking all the time. In the stew pot were beef bouillon cubes (Nestlé Maggi cubes) along with vegetables if the people had some money and meat if they were wealthy. It would cook for hours. For those who couldn't afford meat, the company created a high-protein, soy-based meatlike cube called Maggi Metex, but it took years to make a product that could withstand the hours of cooking the Nigerians did.

Once we thought the product was ready, we brought it into the community. I helped supervise the training of managers and salespeople. Market women (who were the businesspeople of the community) carried baskets of the product through the villages on their heads, and boys on bicycles distributed the product all over town. We wanted everyone around to know how to sell it and how to cook it—specifically that it had to be rehydrated before entering the stew pot.

We projected forty tons of sales in our first year in greater Lagos, and unlike in Japan we moved quickly to get it out there and be number one in the market. By sheer coincidence, the day we launched the product the butchers went on strike, and we ended up selling forty tons in two weeks. Very briefly it felt like a huge win.

Due to rapid sales because of the strike, we failed with our education system and people were eating the product directly out of the box, which, as you can imagine, did not taste good at all.

The demand was so great that there was no time to explain to buyers, many of whom were illiterate, how to prepare the product. Also, one of the most popular local delicacies was a dried beef jerky, and the locals confused our product with that. People bought it in droves, calling it Maggi meat, and there was no time to explain to them what they were eating. After that there were no repeat purchases. It was boom to bust overnight—a total failure. It was the biggest failure of my career.

But I've learned that there are small victories within every failure, including the reward of simply having taken the risk in the first place. Throughout my career I've come to realize that you don't want to chop someone's head off for taking a risk; instead you want to encourage it. If you fail from time to time, and you learn from your mistakes, then you are better prepared the next time.

Failure isn't just a stepping-stone; it's a milestone on the road to future success. At Rank Hovis McDougall and Nestlé International I learned that I can get thrown into a foreign situation and find my way. It was really important to discover that I had enough mental and physical fortitude that I could do well in a situation that was foreign to me.

Traveling around the world and seeing different cultures was also invaluable to my future success. It forced me to have active listening skills, think outside the box regularly, work with people who had different needs, desires, and visions for success, and realize that I can either be someone who just does a job or a person who, while doing a job, is constantly figuring out how to achieve even more.

A lot of people won't be able to fly because they don't know how to fly. This part of my life taught me how to fly and how to maximize my talents. By the time I came back to the United States to work for Nestlé, I had a reputation of being good at what I was doing. It was the first time I arrived at a job with any kind of street cred, and to me that was a huge success.

BYRON: LIGHTING A FIRE

That loss sparked a fire in us. Normally when the season was over, whether we'd won a championship or not, you wouldn't see anyone in the gym for at least a month. The weight room, the basketball court, and the track outside UCLA would all be empty as guys focused on rest. In 1984, when this series against Boston was over, the guys were back working out a week later.

Every Monday through Thursday from 2:00 p.m. to 5:00 p.m., we were working out and playing ball in the gym at UCLA. It wasn't a mandatory workout. It was just who we were. All our guys would be in there, and we'd play against whatever other pros were there—guys like Reggie Theus and LaSalle Thompson. There was a rotating group of about twenty pros and we'd play until we lost, then come back the next day and do it all again for the rest of the summer.

Everybody came to training camp in great shape and looking in mid-season form. Four months after we lost in the NBA Finals, we were still angry and poised to work our butts off to get ready for the season. We decided right then and there that this season, if teams wanted to run with us, we'd run. If they wanted to be physical, we were going to be physical. But no matter what, we were going to play Lakers basketball.

That whole 1985 season, we had a different level of focus. It was basically the same team, but everyone's intensity, conditioning, and drive was sky-high. Most seasons you're not really at your best until after the all-star break, but this season we were there from opening day. We finished the season 62–20—ten games above the next-best team in the conference. It was special. That's really the only way to put it. We were playing on a different level.

We lost only two games in the early rounds of the playoffs before once again meeting the Boston Celtics in the Finals. This time we came out swinging, but we played our game. It was us lifting them off the floor every time we knocked them down. By the end of that series, a lot of their players were talking about how we were dirty and taking cheap shots. Us? The team from Hollywood? What were they talking about? We're a finesse team. We don't play a dirty brand of basketball. We play winning basketball, and that's exactly what we did, beating the Celtics in six and walking away NBA champions on their home court. We didn't hear any celebration that night on the streets outside the Garden, only the sweet sounds of victory in our locker room.

Winning that ring to me was the ultimate because I'd heard all the stories. Eight times the Celtics beat the Lakers in the Finals before we finally beat them in 1985. This wasn't a win only for us, it was also a win for Jerry West and Wilt Chamberlain and all those guys who wanted to get the monkey off their backs. And it was a huge win not just for the players but also for the organization and Lakers fans everywhere. A lot of the other guys had won before, but not like this.

My dad would drive me to the airport for the road games during the playoffs, and when he drove me before game six, he just asked, "So, what do you think?"

"About what?" I asked, with my chick magnet cocker spaniel Roscoe on my lap.

"Games six and seven in Boston."

"Nah, we're gonna win it in six," I said. "It ain't going seven."

After we won, we had a big party that night, and when I came back to Los Angeles the next day, my dad picked me up and stood there looking at me and shaking his head.

"What's wrong, Pops?" I asked.

"You knew you were going to win in six. You said it with so much confidence. How did you know?"

"We were still pissed off from last year, Pop. We weren't going to let it go to seven."

We set our goal and we were focused on a level that we hadn't been able to find the year before—the same players, but with a new-found desire for success. Yes, we were NBA champions in 1985, but only because that championship run began a week after the 1984 season ended.

X's and O's

- Never celebrate until you've crossed the finish line.

- Carry the knowledge learned from mistakes, but don't carry the agony of a loss into the next challenge.

- The learnings from failure can pave the path to future success.

- Learning, growing, and moving ahead in life requires taking risks in spite of fear.

Chapter 4

Fighting Complacency

"When a great team loses through complacency, it will constantly search for new and more intricate explanations to explain away defeat." —Pat Riley

Success can often lead to complacency, especially when it starts to come too easily, but challenging yourself to be greater will take your game to a new level. If you don't, your run at the top won't last very long.

BYRON: ACCEPTING A CHALLENGE

To win at anything in life you have to issue yourself challenges or, if there is a strong leader around, sometimes they can set a challenge for you. Either way, no one just goes out on the court and wins for the sake of winning. There need to be goals and expectations and hurdles to clear.

They can be small and pertain just to you as a player. On the court, maybe you tell yourself you want to average two more rebounds per game this season, or maybe you want to be an all-star.

For the team, the goal is always a championship, but the players need extra challenges to get that ring, especially after they've won one already. In 1985 we had the loss to the Celtics in 1984 that pushed us to glory. Then we lost in 1986 and had that same fire in 1987 to win it once again.

Coach Pat Riley didn't want us getting complacent. He wasn't looking for us to try to win a ring every other year. He knew we had the ability to win every year, but we needed that challenge. As I said before, the second championship is harder to win than the first, because you celebrate for a month or two instead of hitting the gym, claiming you need rest even though odds are you played almost as many games the season before, when you lost. Your mind tricks you into thinking you can take a break.

Our Lakers team was mentally strong. We always strove to win more. We weren't fat cats partying all summer, but we were human, and Riley knew that.

As we were celebrating our 1987 championship at the parade in front of thousands of screaming fans, Riles walked to the microphone and said, "I feel grateful to be part of the team. I feel grateful to be alive and living in Los Angeles. And I'm guaranteeing everybody here, next year we're going to win it again."

Then he just looked back at us and smiled. He hadn't said that just to get the crowd going. That was the master of manipulation lighting a fire under our butts and messing up our vacations all in one breath.

It was definitely calculated. In 1986 we'd lost in the Conference Finals to Ralph Sampson and the Houston Rockets, and Riles had thought we weren't focused—that we played that series with a championship hangover. He remembered that moment better than anyone, so when we beat Boston again in 1987, I think he had already determined that he had to give us a challenge. He knew how to motivate us, and what buttons to push. Back-to-back championships hadn't happened at that point since the Celtics did it in 1968 and 1969, and Riley knew the guarantee was the way to push us to achieve that goal.

When he said it and looked back at us, I was like, *What'd he just say? We're going to win it again? Can't we just enjoy this one for a day or two?*

But you know what? I got home that day and thought about it, and his words stuck in my mind. The next day I went to the gym and looked out at the track, and there were Magic and Coop and A. C. Green. We were getting ready.

CHARLIE: ATTACKING COMPLACENCY

When you dominate in your field, it is human nature to get complacent. Things start to come easy for you, and you take your foot off the gas pedal.

At nearly every stop throughout my career I was brought in to either fix a declining company or sell a new product. I was never hired to maintain the status quo, so I never had time to get complacent. But out in the business world, complacency is everywhere, and there were definitely times throughout my career when it was my job to take advantage of that.

It often happens that the big guy gets satisfied watching his company grow at a slow but steady rate, while innovation is happening at a small company looking to take a piece of the market share.

Let's say the category is growing at 10 percent a year, and every year you're growing at 8 percent a year, and that's terrific because most companies don't grow at 8 percent a year. So you're feeling pretty good about that, but if the category is growing at 10 percent a year, you're actually losing market share every year. You need to be growing at 10 percent just to stay even with the category. So at 8 percent you're losing position and relevance in that category in the eyes of the retailers who are carrying the product, and in the eyes of the consumer.

When that happens, the larger company looks at what's going on with the smaller company and asks if it's worth it to go through the pain of developing something to compete with that smaller company's innovation, or if it's easier to just buy the company.

Usually buying out the smaller company is the easier option—and that was my goal when I was the chairman of the board at Day Runner, a company that sells daily, weekly, and monthly planners and other professional planning accessories. With Day Runner we didn't want to stay in it long-term to be fighting with the big guys, but rather to fix the company, make it profitable, and get out and sell it to a competitor as fast as possible, because the category was declining.

People were moving away from paper-based organizer/planners and relying more on the calendars on their cell phones and computers, so we knew we had to make a move fast. It's harder to grow share in a declining category. It makes more sense to take a company that's losing money, figure out why it's losing money, turn it around, and make it an acquisition target for someone.

Day planners were still popular, and if we could sell an efficient assortment of products, we could make a quick profit. When you see an opportunity, you have to jump at it. There is some risk, but the reward is much greater.

BYRON: CALLING GUYS OUT

Those old enough to remember may know that Riley's challenge worked: we won the championship again in 1988. The idea of issuing challenges and making bold statements stayed with me, and I pulled a page from the Pat Riley book of motivation myself at the start of the 1993–94 season.

I was a free agent and parting with the Lakers for the first time when Larry Brown, who was coaching the Indiana Pacers, called me. He was in LA and gave me a ticket to come to watch them play the Clippers. After the game I stood there outside the locker room and waited for him to come outside.

"Listen, we want to sign you and we need two things from you: your leadership and your scoring," he said when we met face-to-face. "Can you provide those two things for us?"

"Absolutely."

I felt comfortable and confident saying that because of my time with the Lakers. I'd won championships, so I knew exactly what a leader should look like and what he should do. Going to Indiana with a young team that had never been past the first round, I knew I had to just go in there and be myself—play hard, give advice, and be supportive. If there's a guy in practice I need to get on, then I'll get on him. I was coming in with credibility, so I knew they'd respect me.

Reggie Miller was the star of that team, and his talent was through the roof, but he wasn't that vocal a leader. He would say little things here and there, but he didn't get on guys the way others would. He was also one of those guys who do just enough in practice to be ready for the game. He worked, but he didn't go 150 miles per hour. He just practiced. He was always ready for the game, but the guys following his lead, who were maybe less talented, would not be as ready.

So right away I wanted to give the guys a challenge, because I knew that if you challenge a guy like Reggie, he can take it to another level. When I got off the plane in Indiana, a bunch of news reporters met me at the airport, and they said, "Wow, you brought a lot of luggage."

"I plan on being here for a couple of years."

"What are your expectations of this team?" someone asked.

"Eastern Conference Finals," I said confidently.

"The guys have never been out of the first round," the reporter replied.

"I'm looking at Reggie Miller, Rik Smits, the Davis boys— Antonio and Dale—Derrick McKey. We got the talent. We can do it."

That was it. I put it out there. That was leadership before even leaving the airport. I issued them a challenge, and now we all had to live up to it. I saw the talent from afar and I wanted them to know right away that I had confidence in them. And just as with Riley, it worked.

CHARLIE: THE RIGHT MESSAGE SELLS

In my line of work I didn't have the ability to issue big public challenges, mainly because who would listen? I could set goals for people and rally the troops with incentives, but I couldn't just shout, "We're all going to be rich" and watch the people below me work their hardest to make that happen.

What I did to fight complacency when I was in the bottled water industry was instill innovation. Positive change brings out the winner in most players, and my go-to change was almost always in marketing.

There was always a lot of resistance to marketing, because the water industry people were set in their ways and often resistant to change. At Sparkletts, for instance, most of the new business, before I got there, was based on the route sales reps' knocking on doors and getting new customers to try the service. It was an inexpensive sales tactic, but it was hardly innovative. People have been knocking on doors since the beginning of time, and I knew that in order to keep that edge we needed to do something different.

I brought Kathleen Torrell in, and we started doing a ton of direct response television. It was the most expensive way to get an account, but it had the highest return on investment because the customer stayed longer and we gave no free trials. We did credit screenings on every single customer, and we tracked how we had gotten that customer and what the return was. By far the highest return was from our advertising.

Sparkletts had a great image with the "Sparkletts Man" and the shiny disco ball–like backs of the trucks, so the marketing was strictly about getting people to try the product. It was hard-hitting direct response, and our systems were so sophisticated that we knew if our spot at three o'clock on *The Oprah Winfrey Show* had paid out, because people would be calling within twenty-four hours. If a spot didn't work, we would simply cancel the next spots on that particular show.

At Deer Park we didn't have those tools in place, and a lot of the advertising dollars in the company were going toward retail, so we hired a boutique ad agency called Jordan, Case and McGrath in New York, and they came up with the campaign slogan "Deer Park, that's good water."

Oftentimes the simplest ads are the ones that people remember most. We did multiple spots, some of which were crazy. In the beginning I needed to be convinced because, honestly, I was not an out-of-the-box thinker when I started out. I wasn't sure about needing cutting-edge advertising that broke through all the commercials so people would remember our product. But I trusted the copywriter,

Gene Case, who was brilliant and just nailed it. There was one commercial that showed two boxers fighting. One of them got knocked out, and when he woke up, he drank the water and said, "Deer Park, that's good water." It was classic. These are things people remember and, in the end, these ads made millions of dollars for Deer Park.

BYRON: LOSING THE EDGE

In 1989—before I left the Lakers—we were itching for the famous Pat Riley "three-peat" that I hopefully don't have to pay him to mention in this book. Winning is hardest, though, when it starts to come too easy.

We still had the hearts of champions, but the fire that we'd had after my rookie-season loss to the Celtics was not burning as strongly. We were again the number one seed coming out of the West, and we dominated the first three rounds of the playoffs, sweeping the Trail Blazers, SuperSonics, and Suns to enter the NBA Finals 11–0 in the playoffs. But it was our fifth trip to the Finals in six years, so winning had just sort of become the norm. Complacency was definitely setting in.

There was one game in the early rounds that was a bit of foreshadowing of what was to come. In game four of the Western Conference Semifinals, we were on the road in Seattle, up 3–0, trying to close out the Sonics.

We came out flat, and we were down twenty points by the end of the first quarter and as many as twenty-six in the first half. As a veteran team we didn't panic, and we certainly weren't going to be the type of team to just lie down and tell ourselves we'd get it next time.

That wasn't the Lakers style, and it certainly wasn't how Pat Riley coached. His mentality was that we were up 3–0 and we had our foot on their necks, so we should press it down and not let it up. That's how we all saw closeout games. It was our chance to put the dagger in them.

The other team, though, has nothing to lose. They're playing stress-free basketball. Any opponent down 3–0 is going to give it everything they've got. They don't want to be embarrassed and get swept, so they come out guns blazing.

But we were champions, and we knew that the we-can-lose-this-and-win-it-at-home-next-game mentality is for losers. Champions don't take that kind of risk. Champions think, *If we close them out, then we get more rest and more time to prepare for the next team.* You also don't let up because if the opponent spots a weakness or makes a big adjustment that works, you can go from 3–0 to 3–2 or 3–3 real quick. Plus, most of the guys had been around the league long enough at that point to know that injuries can happen at any moment, so fewer games equals less chance of something bad happening.

So, being down twenty after the first quarter was a big deficit to overcome, but we were going to try our hardest to make it happen. Riley was on us, but he was still as calm as could be. To him it was just the first quarter, and the game isn't won in one quarter. We still had thirty-six minutes to play, so we would just chip away.

Magic was the guy who always looked ahead at the numbers. He would say, "Let's get it under fifteen," "Let's get it to ten," "Let's get it to six"—whatever it was, he just wanted that number lower so that by halftime we would be in great shape.

The winning mentality starts on the defensive end. We could always hit shots, but the focus and determination comes in with defense, where there is less glory. It doesn't feel as good to see the other team miss as it does to score yourself, but it counts just the same, so the focus has to be just as strong. Winners are defense minded. They care about both ends of the court, especially when they're down.

The Sonics came out hot and played with such a high intensity that we knew sooner or later they would tire out if we just stayed the course. Eventually we started to slow them down, got them to miss shots, and turned misses into fast breaks. Continuing to push, and never deviating from the plan, we went into the half down eleven, shaved off three more after the third, and outscored them by ten in the fourth to win the game 97–95 and end the series.

But as I said, that game was a bit of foreshadowing of what was to come. When you get to the Finals year after year, you never expect anything to go wrong. But when a team starts to get complacent, the basketball gods step in, and bad luck starts to happen. It's a recipe for disaster.

That's what happened to us in the Finals. I pulled my hamstring in practice the night before game one, Magic got hurt in game two, and we just fell apart as a team, getting swept by the Pistons in four games.

We'd stopped challenging ourselves. We'd stopped reaching for even greater goals. We'd stopped finding new ways to motivate ourselves to that next level. And so we lost. Kareem retired after the season, and new challenges were on the horizon.

CHARLIE: LITTLE GUY TACTICS

You have a real competitive spirit when you're trying to beat the big guy. You're more nimble. You think about things that you're going to try that a large company may not want to take a chance on. You have that nothing-to-lose mentality. It can be fun just to be in the battle. That's what Byron was up against after he and the Lakers won a few championships. Everyone was out to take them down, mainly because it feels great to knock out the champs.

In business it's exactly the same. When you start taking share from somebody else and you're winning in the marketplace, an excitement grows among the team. It's easy to motivate people when they are watching the numbers climb.

At Day Runner, every month we would get the new share reports, and every month the whole organization knew how were we doing against our competition. There may have been two or three other companies relevant to us, then a lot of really small ones. Our goal was to be taking share away from those relevant competitors. As we continued to do that, everyone was proud.

On months that it didn't work, we had to explain why it hadn't and how things were going to change. It could be because the competition had run a ridiculously expensive program. When everybody is more or less at the same price, and one company offers a two-dollar-per-case discount for a month, the stores will buy a lot more of that product. Then they'll display it more because they're able to show a much lower price on the end-aisle display or a wing display. If you know that, you can justify your performance, but over the course of the year we wanted to be up.

There are easy ways to turn things around. If the leader in the market has, let's say, a forty share, and the number two company starts cutting its prices to get more shelf space, the number two company can sell more just by taking away one or two facings from a competitor and increasing its share. It costs the leader in the market more to match because the leader is doing it on three times as many cases as the little guy. But if it does nothing, the leader slowly loses its lead.

It's the equivalent to a coach on the top team in the NBA resting his starters with a twenty-point lead in the fourth quarter. The other team will make a bit of a comeback, and even if the favored team wins, the margin of victory is smaller and the coach was forced to change his plan to secure victory. It's irritating if the coach has to put his starters back in the game to make it happen.

That's what this is for the big guy: irritating. It forces it to change its business plan. After it loses share, it has options. Sometimes the leader will say, "We are going to squash them, because we can afford to do more than they can." Or sometimes it'll say, "Let's just buy them and get them out of the marketplace."

Once we irritated the market at Day Runner, we had negotiations with the number one. At one point we were even thinking of trying to buy it, but it had too many issues with its labor force that we didn't want to take on. But as it turned out, we ended up making enough noise in the industry that we sold to a huge paper goods company that had a lot of synergy with us but was not competing directly with us in the space. Twenty months after paying $12 million with a private equity firm, we sold Day Runner for $45 million. We got four times our money out in just twenty months because we saw some star players resting on the bench and we took advantage.

X's and O's

- New challenges will help keep a champion from getting complacent.

- You have to remain equally focused on winning from start to finish or else the competition will find a way to beat you.

- You learn as much from a poorly run team as from a successful one.

- Innovation in a stagnant market is a powerful tool for success.

Chapter 5

We Win, We All Win

"Alone we can do so little; together we can do so much." —Helen
Keller

Everyone on the team plays a role in the success of an organization,
and every player has to take pride in knowing that putting the team
first is the only way to be a champion. Money can be a motivator, but
respect and appreciation are what really drive people.

BYRON: THE BENEFITS OF TEAM SUCCESS

During our run in the eighties, the Los Angeles Lakers were
successful for one reason and one reason only: we played for each
other. Everyone on the team did whatever was necessary to win each
game, and then each playoff series, and eventually, in three of my
years there, the championship.

We put money and ego and stats aside and focused solely on winning rings. Every game, certain people made sacrifices and others
rose to the occasion. Every season there were different leaders con-
tributing on different levels.

One of those championship years, I was the team's leading scorer for the season. Casual NBA fans might not remember that, because it didn't matter to us, so we weren't out there talking about who did what. Other seasons I was asked to contribute in different ways.

The same is true with everyone else on the team. Magic would play every position from point guard to center based on who was hurt or what was needed. Kurt Rambis was one of those guys who did all the dirty work. Riley told him his job was to take the ball out of bounds and get it to Magic, where he would banana cut and catch it on the run. I don't remember one time that that ball hit the floor. Kurt would grab it out of the bottom of the net, step behind the line, and send it to Magic. That was his job, and he was the best in the league at it. As far as I'm concerned that made him a great leader, because it helped the team win but didn't show up on the stat sheet.

Stats equal money, and for a lot of players money is a big motivator. There are special players in this league who play because they love the game, and because they want to win championships, but nowadays most guys play because they want to get paid. Guys who are on the last year of their contract and trying to be more aggressive from a selfish standpoint are not helping the team. As a coach you have to pull them aside as soon as you pick up on it, and say, "I know that your contract is up and I know you're trying to get paid, but you're going about it the wrong way."

Magic had a little saying that he told me my rookie year and that stuck with me, and it was sort of the motto that we lived by as a team. He'd say, "We win, we all win."

It was five simple words that rang true throughout my career. "We win, we all win." If the Lakers win a championship, then everybody gets rewarded. No one worried about individual stats, because our feeling was that if the team stinks, playing well as an individual is not going to benefit you. When you win a championship, everyone on the team from top to bottom benefits.

In my rookie year we lost to the Celtics in the Finals, but the next year, when we beat them, everybody in LA wanted us to make appearances—autograph sessions, store openings, commercials, everything. It went from the first guy, Magic, down to the twelfth guy. Everyone made money that summer.

Magic couldn't be everywhere all the time, mainly because these companies couldn't afford him, so then my phone would ring or James Worthy's or Coop's. Everyone benefited.

A lot of players today don't get it. They have a me-first attitude and they say, "This is a business." They point to teams that are willing to cut them or trade them without an ounce of loyalty and tell themselves (and anyone else who will listen) that they have to put themselves and their families first because that's what the team would do.

That's not what the team would do. That might be what an owner does as an individual or a GM does as an individual, but that's not what the team does. Teams win together.

CHARLIE: GOING ALL IN

For most of my career I had a lot to lose in everything I was doing because I was largely working with new products, new ventures, or major changes. I was never taking an existing business and just trying to keep it stable. I was always stepping into a situation where I had a ton of skin in the game, so I wanted to make everyone else have skin in the game too. I wanted them to have the same attitude that I had: that we had to fix it because we had our own money at stake.

At Nestlé I had a number of jobs, but eventually ended up running a small water company called Deer Park. In three years I took the business from losing 40 percent of sales at net operating profit to a positive cash flow and a breakeven at net profit. I couldn't squeeze any more water out of that stone, so I went to my superiors and told them we had two options: we could invest heavily or sell the company.

Prior to my arrival, my predecessor had moved away from the Teamsters Union and created independent owner-operators to deliver the water, and used copackers rather than self-manufacturing. I provided a full business plan for how the investment would work and what I could do with full control of all aspects of the operation, including signing a new collective bargaining agreement with the Teamsters Union, but my superiors decided to sell.

At that point I estimated that Deer Park was worth maybe $13 to $15 million, but there was so much concern about buying a company that needed a new collective bargaining agreement with the Teamsters Union that nobody wanted to pay anything near that. The price got so low that I decided that I should just buy the business. My two partners and I ended up buying the company for $3.5 million, with one partner putting in $500,000 in cash and another putting up his house as collateral in order to get a bank loan for $3 million. I gave up my Nestlé career to run the company, so when I say we had skin in the game I mean it. The company was now ours.

We made a commitment to fix the company by getting a new collective bargaining agreement with the Teamsters Union, expanding by lowering the quit rate, and servicing the customers better. But taking Deer Park private, and no longer having the mother Nestlé to provide us with capital, was something we had to let employees know was going to be good for them.

I energized the team by explaining that we now had very good partnerships with Wissahickon Spring Water Company and Tyler

Mountain Water, and that we had the technology and skill sets we needed. I told them we had the union agreeing to a new collective bargaining agreement so we could control the movements of the route drivers. We had the funding from the bank to expand, and most importantly we were now all owners.

Employees got stock commensurate with their position in the organization, which we'd never had at Nestlé. I had to explain how their options were gaining value, because some people didn't get it. But the fact of the matter was that, even as union employees, I wanted them to feel they were as important as anyone else—that their loyalty couldn't be to the union, it had to be to the company. By giving them stock in the company, which was really a phantom stock, we showed them that if the company did well, then they would do better than just through their hourly union contract. That was extremely important.

Did I know categorically that everyone was going to be rich? No. Was I nervous about it? Absolutely. But I knew it would motivate the team to be at their best and do what was best for the company. Mostly, though, if my partners and I won, I wanted the whole team to win.

BYRON: ACKNOWLEDGING THE HOT HAND

Part of winning together and playing unselfish basketball is acknowledging who has the hot hand, and on more than one occasion, Magic, Kareem, Coop, and I turned to Big Game James to lead us to the promised land.

In the 1988 Finals—our third championship run during my tenure—we were playing the Detroit Pistons. Heading into that series we swept the Spurs in the first round but had to win a game seven against both Utah and Dallas to make it to the Finals.

The Pistons were tough. Every possession was a battle and we were running on fumes, so as a team we really had to dig deep when it came time to play a game seven against them as well.

In that series James Worthy led the team in scoring in every one of our wins, but that game seven was something special. He was doing everything on both ends of the floor, and once we recognized that he was in a different zone, the rest of us did everything possible to get him open. My job in that game was to set screens for James. I was great at setting screens, so I was trying to knock people's heads off just to get him open. Magic was going to be the one with the ball in his hands, so I wasn't going to be able to facilitate in that way. Instead I used my body and helped off the ball to make sure James was taking the shots.

It's team basketball, and for what it's worth I still scored a quiet twenty-one points that night—proving that when you do what it takes to win, even on the court we all win.

Anyway, by the second half James was just on a different planet. Neither Dennis Rodman nor John Salley could guard him. He was on a mission. As teammates we let him know that we noticed what was happening. At every break I'd say, "I'm going to keep setting screens for you. Just keep getting open." Magic, Kareem—they kept pushing him too. None of this took away from our regular game plan. It wasn't just "Let's let James do everything." It was recognizing that our path to a championship would go through the hot hand.

He finished that game with thirty-six points, sixteen rebounds, and ten assists—the first triple-double of his career. To have that in game seven of the NBA Finals and lead the Lakers to another championship is what winning is all about. To this day it's still one of the greatest single-game performances of all time. He was the Finals MVP and will forever be Big Game James.

CHARLIE: BUILDING THE BANDWAGON

I believed in the Deer Park name, and the "Deer Park, that's good water" marketing slogan proved to be a success. For me, the most important asset in any company is the brand name. You've got to treasure that brand name because it stands for something that's meaningful to the consumer. So now we owned the name Deer Park, and it was worth a whole lot more than we'd bought it for. That was a cause for celebration, and the team needed to know that. We were celebrating our independence. We were a new company and the sky was the limit. Get on the bandwagon because we're going to take this for a great ride.

You want to get people excited about it. You have to paint the picture of the new vision and the new goals, and everyone has to play their part because each member of the team is just as important as the next.

I believed in the team—from the frontline people to top management. Before we did the deal I had gone to a couple of guys named Tim and Lon, who were the heads of the Teamsters Union local and definitely knew people who knew people who could break your legs if things didn't go according to plan.

I told them I had the opportunity to buy the company but I wouldn't buy it unless we could agree on a framework for a new collective bargaining agreement. I wanted to buy back all the route trucks, have employees again, and pay them a certain amount per bottle delivered and returned.

Smoking a cigar and listening to my proposition in his little office, Tim blew cigar smoke in my face and said, "OK, the first contract is yours, but if you don't deliver, you are mine."

Pressure? What pressure?

We did the deal and moved forward with our goal to expand down the Atlantic Seaboard and bring the Deer Park name from Maine to Florida. We weren't going to be a $8 million company. We were going to be a $25 million company. That was our goal for the next three years, to get from $8 million to $25 million.

As it turned out, we didn't need that long. In a period of twenty months we went from $8 million to $12 million and sold the company to Clorox for forty times our invested capital. We'd bought it for $3.5 million, paying half a million in cash and taking bank loans for the balance, and we sold it for over $20 million in twenty months.

Everyone benefited, and most people were shocked by it. A secretary might get a check for $10K because of that sale. It was a huge, championship-level victory for the organization.

BYRON: ON THE STRING

Unselfish basketball wins championships. I may not touch the ball a few times down the court, but I still have to run the floor, I still have to set the screen. I still have to keep my spacing. You have that mentality because you want to win. And if Worthy was rolling, that was my job. With the team that we had, no one ever thought, *I haven't touched the ball in a while.* It was more like *This guy's playing great, so let's get him the ball.* That's just who we were as basketball players. It was all about the team, and never about the individual.

That's what basketball is all about. Everybody has to do their part or it doesn't work. One guy is not going to win the game for you every single night. It's got to be a combination of everybody being on the same page and moving. All those parts have to move simultaneously. It's like tying everybody up with a string. If one part of that string moves, everybody better move with it.

As a coach I always talk about that in huddles, in film sessions, and in practice. Be on the string. It's the same thing on defense as well. You've got to be on the string at all times if you want to be rewarded with a victory.

CHARLIE: CREATING INCENTIVES

There are all sorts of ways to provide incentive and push for people to "be on the string" within the company. At McKesson Corp. we had a five-point performance evaluation system, and ranking would drive promotions and salary increases. Every job had a certain grade, and each grade had a certain salary scale associated with it—a minimum and a maximum. If an employee was below the midpoint salary for the grade of his or her job, that would enable the supervisor to propose a higher salary increase from one year to the next, depending upon how the employee did within the job. Every operating unit within McKesson operated with that system, not just the water company.

It was a very good system that was tied to both annual salary increase and bonuses. The bonuses were a function of how each group did against its budget, how the company did, and how individuals performed in agreed-upon improvement activities for them. So the bonus plan had three parts. The percentages varied depending on how much a division really drove the profits of the whole company. If it drove a high percentage of the profits, the corporate goals were a higher percentage of the bonus pool than for other divisions that drove lower percentages.

For example, if I'm your supervisor and you're working for us in a French-speaking part of Canada, but you don't speak French, then I might have as a goal for you that you have to learn French. You have to take a certain number of courses and you have to move from course A to course B, and 20 percent of your total bonus is going to be predicated on your mastering French. If you do, you get it. If you don't, you don't get it. In your division, half of the remaining bonus is tied to how you do against your profit plan, and the other half is how the total corporation does. These goals are set a year in advance, and during the course of the year you know how you're doing. In a lot of companies you have no clue what your bonus is going to be. Here you have total visibility of how the company is doing, how your division is doing, and how you're doing against your personal goals.

My feeling was always that I want to pay you the most I can pay you, so we didn't stop at 100 percent with bonuses. If you made more than 100 percent of the profit you had been expecting, your bonus scaled up to as much as 150 percent of the original figure. So if you were making a base of $100K a year with a 20 percent bonus potential, you could actually make 50 percent more, or a $30K bonus, if you exceeded your budget by an agreed-upon percentage. It was very good and very motivational for people.

BYRON: THE VALUE OF APPRECIATION

There's nothing wrong with wanting to get paid, and it is human nature to let the stats motivate play, because stats equal money. If some guys come out and play hard every night because of it, then great. As a coach I'll give a player that personal win if it's the fourth quarter and we're up by twenty points, and he has twenty-five points, thirteen rebounds, and nine assists. I'll say to the player, "Hey, you're one assist short of a triple-double, do you want to go back in?" As a former player I know how hard it is to get a triple-double, so I want to give the guy that option.

In the game, though, he's not thinking about how a triple-double might lead to more money down the road. He's thinking he worked hard and that he knows the coaches and the fans will appreciate that achievement.

People want to be appreciated. That's the main incentive for success. As a coach, when we're watching tape, I'll point something out and say, "You didn't get the shot, but you made the play. You got him there wide open on the shot because you ran the floor. You got him because you set the screen." We try to bring those things to players' attention because you want each of them to know that he played a part in the win.

But it is a business, and it would have been James's right to want to be the star somewhere else, and pack his bags the way James Harden did when he left Oklahoma City for Houston. Players do it all the time, and when teams lose, the trade rumors circulate, so it's only fair.

James and I both went through it almost every year. One time there was talk that James would go to Dallas for Mark Aguirre, who was an all-star and a friend of Magic Johnson's. The media made the connection because it was a good story, but had it happened, Magic would have had nothing to do with it. But James got calls from his agent, who was hearing the buzz, and he was rightfully upset.

He marched up to owner Jerry Buss's office and demanded, "Are you trading me or what?"

Jerry Buss, being Jerry Buss, said as calmly as could be, "James, if we're going to trade you, I'll let you know."

Dr. Buss was a straight shooter, and if he did trade you, he would be the one to come down and tell you. He would never blindside a player, so for James, no news was good news in that meeting. But Dr. Buss was also great at telling you what you meant to the organization

and how being a Laker meant being part of the family. He appreciated every one of us, and that always went a long way. That's why
the players all stayed as long as we did. And for his efforts, James
was a three-time champion, seven-time all-star, and the NBA Finals
MVP in 1988—so his mind-set was probably similar to mine when
my name got tossed around in trade rumors: *If you trade me, this is
what you're going to be missing.*

All that stuff went out the window once the ball was tipped each
night. Then we were five guys on the court playing for each other.
We were five guys on a string with the incentive that if we win, we
all win. That's all that ever mattered.

CHARLIE: EVERYONE IS A PARTNER

I actually don't think that money is the number one motivator. I
think feeling valued is far and away the most important thing. I
don't want to be in a job where people aren't listening to what I'm
saying, don't really care about what I'm saying, and don't value my
contribution. If I'm really valued, as long as I feel that I'm being paid
fairly, I am not going to run to the next job. Even if I can get 20
percent more money, I'm probably not going to leave. There has to
be something else that's driving me to want to look elsewhere, and
that tends to be that people aren't honest with me, or they are taking
advantage of me, or I'm not being treated fairly or rewarded fairly.

At McKesson the raise and bonus structure was good financially,
but it also made people feel good about their work and their progress. We didn't just come in and demand these goals. We talked with
employees, and often they created their own goals. They knew how
much their divisions had brought in the year before, and they knew
what could be changed to increase that number. It was more of a

conversation, because if somebody has been in a job for a while, and we have an honest relationship, I don't think that I'm going to get sandbagged and they don't think they're going to be taken advantage of.

After a couple of years you know which people are really pushing to do the best they can, and which ones are holding back and not giving their all. You want people to feel that they know what's happening in the organization, that they can make a difference in the organization, and that if they do, they'll be rewarded for it.

At Deer Park it was the same thing. We didn't give people stock options to throw away money. We wanted them to want to win, and we wanted them to feel appreciated—to know that their hard work as a team was paying off. Everyone had skin in the game, and no matter what an individual's job was, everyone was invested in the success of the company. I treated the union people and the Teamsters' reps as partners, not as workers. Partnership is important. Just ask Tim and Lon.

X's and O's

- The guy doing the dirty work is just as important as the guy hitting the big shots.

- Honesty from the top down will allow people to perform at their best and know that their contributions are meaningful.

- The best motivation is appreciation.

- The entire organization must understand and embrace the vision in order for the team to be successful.

Chapter 6

Winner Mentality versus Loser Mentality

"Winning is the most important thing in my life, after breathing. Breathing first, winning next." —George Steinbrenner

It's easy to give up when times get tough, when it seems there's no chance for victory, but a true leader fights to live another day and ultimately comes out on top. The players who don't give it their all, or look around and don't smell success, never had a shot to begin with.

BYRON: FIGHTING EXTRAORDINARY CIRCUMSTANCES

The start of the nineties was tough for us. Cap retired, and the next season we got upset by the Phoenix Suns and missed the Conference Finals for the first time in nine years. After that, Coach Riley resigned, eventually landing in New York with the Knicks. We muscled our way to the Finals again in that 1990–91 season under Coach Mike Dunleavy, but the whole landscape was changing.

That year we lost to Michael Jordan and the Chicago Bulls in the Finals, and as a player on the court, I could just tell that was the start of something special for that team. Michael Jordan, when it comes to leadership, was a taskmaster. I heard he would get into fights in practice and push guys to the limit, but his competitive fire was unmatched by anyone in the league. When they beat us in that series, it just felt like a turning point.

To me, though, as long as we had Magic we always had a chance. We had talented guys like Sam Perkins, Vlade Divac, and Larry Drew on the team, and while the atmosphere was different, the potential was there as long as Magic was there to push these guys and lead the team. With him on the roster and the talent we had, I always felt we still had a chance to compete for a championship.

But at the very beginning of the 1991–92 season, Magic announced he had HIV and was retiring. I actually heard it on the radio first, on my way home, and I just sat in disbelief with my ex-wife. Then, when he came to the locker room the next day and told us, I put my head down and started to cry.

He walked around the room and hugged everybody and said, "I'm going to beat this. I'm going to be fine."

But I didn't know what to make of it. When I was hugging him, my little bit of knowledge of HIV at the time was saying that he wasn't going to be around for much longer. In that moment I thought that not only was I losing the best teammate I'd ever had, but I was also losing a friend. He had a different attitude, though, and when he went out to do the press conference, he stood up and was as strong as anybody I've ever seen.

Anytime you lose a player like Magic Johnson, one of the best players in the history of the game, you know that your team's talent is definitely taking a dip. You're not going to get another guy on that level to take his place. Every time he walked on the court there was a possibility of his having a triple-double, so we were missing that element. James Worthy, A. C. Green, and I were still thinking championships. After years of winning it was ingrained in our minds. But when we started playing those games without Magic, we looked around and the realization set in that we were not that championship-caliber team.

Being "just a playoff team" wasn't something that worked in Los Angeles, and we all had to push ourselves to make it even that far. Once you accept losing, though, there's no turning back. Once you've told yourself you can't win a championship, any obstacle will find a way to knock you down. That season—the 1991–92 season—we were the eighth seed and facing the Portland Trail Blazers in the first round. We were down 2–1, with a chance to tie it up at home, when after game three we turned on the TVs and saw madness on the streets of LA.

The verdict in the Rodney King trial had come in, and Los Angeles was rioting. When I left the Forum and got in my car, it was just pandemonium. People were going crazy, looting and tearing up the city. A white friend of mine was at that game, and on his way home he was pulled from his car by a couple of black guys and beaten up. His son was in the car with him.

Everybody was angry. I was angry. They had the tape. Four policemen standing there with batons beating the shit out of King, and nobody was being held accountable? Nobody was being prosecuted? It didn't make sense to us. Well, actually it made total sense, and that was the problem.

The Forum in Inglewood was just too dangerous a place to play, so they moved the next game to the Thomas & Mack Center in Nevada. As a team we weren't mentally tough enough to handle losing our home court advantage or playing on the road when our families were back in the middle of chaos, so we lost that game and the series.

The next season we were the eighth seed again, and went up 2–0 against the Phoenix Suns. They came back to win it in five. We had lost the magic.

CHARLIE: EXPLAINING CHANGE FIRSTHAND

If you're making major changes to a culture, some employees don't want to let go of the past, and they're always comparing the present negatively to the good old days. Back then their company was failing, but their lives were easier, they weren't working as hard, and there wasn't as much pressure. So to them, those were better times.

At some point, if your people can't let go of the past, they won't be able to embrace the present or the prospect of the future. As a leader you have to paint a picture for them and explain why change is necessary. If you can't get them to understand why they need this change, they'll never work with a winning mentality. At some point you have to stop honoring the past, and start honoring the success that the present has enabled.

The past, present, and future of the bottled water industry were always the route drivers. They were on the front line dealing directly with the customer. They were the players, and at both Deer Park and McKesson Water I wanted my team of drivers to be packed with Magic Johnsons, Kareem Abdul-Jabbars, and Byron Scotts.

Most of the route sales reps were former athletes, actually, who were very goal oriented and competitive. So if somebody averaged 150 bottles a day and got 170 one day, that excited people. Each person had a defined geographic area to work in, and drivers could grow their particular geographic area until they maxed out the number of bottles they could transport. Those who were really successful would go back to reload and thought about it as a game of "How much I can get done in a day?" I loved to be part of that game and that goal of really just knocking the socks off the business each day.

At both Deer Park and McKesson Water I made a point of riding along with the route sales reps and delivering half the bottles myself, so I could put myself in their shoes when making broad company decisions, and also so I could watch my players perform. I required all my managers to do the same. If you don't have the best players, you're not going to win the game, and it helps to be out there with them in the fight from time to time.

As I quickly learned, it was not an easy job. I went one day with one of the New York City route sales reps at Deer Park to service Grand Central Terminal, where some of the water coolers were down on the platforms by the trains. The ramps going down to the platform were pretty steep. I probably should have noticed that ahead of time, but instead I had a runaway dolly. I lost control of it going down the ramp and had glass bottles and crates breaking on the way down as they fell off the dolly.

Another time, in my typical fashion, I wanted to deliver more water than the sales rep had originally planned, so I tried to beat the system by asking my route partner to pull the truck right to the entrance of Grand Central Terminal. He ended up getting a parking ticket and then a second ticket, and the truck was about to get towed when we came back. I paid the tickets, and it's safe to say my days delivering to Grand Central Terminal were over. It was really embarrassing, but more importantly it was proof that not everyone could do the job.

To keep the winning going we needed a fleet full of all-stars at all times. When our team was top notch we were winning, but that wasn't always the case at either of the water companies.

BYRON: FIGHTING EXPECTED FAILURE

The Lakers fizzled out in the nineties. Losing became an option, and the team started to accept it. As I said, you don't recover from that until you find a Kobe Bryant or a Shaquille O'Neal to breathe new life into the organization.

A few years later, when I got taken in the expansion draft by the Vancouver Grizzlies, losing wasn't just an option, it was expected—and that just wasn't my style.

My first reaction when I heard they'd taken me was, *Damn, I'm done.* It was my thirteenth year in the league, and I had never missed the playoffs, but first-year franchises never win championships, so this was going to be a struggle.

I knew that, but I wanted to go in with a positive attitude. As the senior guy and the only one on that team who had won championships, I knew that my voice would carry some weight. Right from the start of training camp I tried to get the team to realize that I lived to play in May. I wanted all of them to know that we still could have a pretty good team if everybody was on the same page. I was always a very positive person, and I thought that if we played together, anything was possible.

For the most part, my pep talks were not being heard. We had some veterans who wanted to win, like Greg Anthony, Kenny Gattison, and Blue Edwards, but the young guys had a loser mentality. The team started off with two wins, but then we lost nineteen straight and just fell apart from there. For the first time in my career I was on a team at the bottom of the standings.

It was like a tug-of-war with the young guys, trying to get them to try to win. Greg and I would push and try to get them to understand what it takes to win consistently, but it would fall on deaf ears.

It led to fights in the locker room. Guys just didn't get along. They wouldn't accept the fact that we veterans were trying to help them by being a little hard on them.

There was one incident when Greg Anthony and Antonio Harvey got into a fistfight in the locker room. Greg couldn't take it anymore. He was a fiery guy and even had his hand wrapped up because of an injury, but he unwrapped it, stood up, had a few words with Antonio, and just punched him. It had to happen. When they don't listen, and it goes in one ear and out the other, sometimes a physical altercation is the only thing that seems to get their attention.

I'm more of a calm leader. I keep my composure almost always. But Greg—he had no problem starting and finishing fights.

When you're a winner, you're a winner. You cannot tone that down when you're used to winning. Every night we wanted to at least go out there and give it everything we had. If you've been winning all your life, that's just something that's instilled in you, and you're going to keep pushing to keep trying to win every single night no matter what.

These other guys, they didn't get it. From the second they joined the team they had been hanging their heads on the court and partying off the court because they didn't give a damn about basketball.

It was a bad situation for rookies like Bryant Reeves. Big Country, as he was called, was big and talented, but he didn't love basketball the way you need to in order to be successful. Being on this team was poison for a guy like him.

For me it was depressing. I started drinking beer for the first time in my life. After one of the early losses, Kenny Gattison and Greg handed me a Coors Light and said, "Here, you need to have a cold one." Before I knew it I was popping open a few at home after every game.

That's how I dealt with it. It was that tough. When I was out in public or at the games I was still going to be as positive as possible, but at home I was drowning my sorrows. I'd still be the first one to the gym every morning, but I was also the last one on his couch at night.

When a team doesn't want to win, there's really nothing you can do. Someone has to go, and in this case it was I.

CHARLIE: OVERCOMING A FAILING CULTURE

When I first got to Deer Park, the company was losing 40 percent of sales at net operating profit because in an effort to get away from the Teamsters Union, Nestlé had closed down the manufacturing facility and the route drivers' operation in the South Bronx. The company did this on a Friday night with no notice to the unions at all. It had gone to a distribution organization called Leaseway Transportation, which had promised Nestlé it could do all the deliveries with independent drivers who owned their own vehicles and would operate with independent routes. Then Nestlé took the manufacturing to a copacker and essentially shut down everything except marketing, sales, and administrative functions, which were set up in an office in Rockland County, New York.

Leaseway hired back all the original route drivers as independent owner-operators, so you had very unhappy people who had never owned and operated their own trucks before. Deer Park was on an old IBM System/3 computer system, which was a card system, and in the process of shutting down the South Bronx operation it lost all the customer files, so the only ones who knew where the customers were located were the original route drivers.

All of a sudden the company had all sorts of problems with

outstanding receivables because the salespeople didn't know how to bill. It was a mess.

Forget about championships, at that point we weren't even a play-off team. At Deer Park we were largely in retail grocery, and we had maybe twenty routes. At McKesson Water, at our peak, when I was running it, we ended up having 750,000 customers on likely more than a thousand routes. There we had different problems.

In an effort to jump-start growth, my predecessor had approved a program in which customers got several months free for signing a contract. We got an enormous amount of business, but there was no credit screening and we had huge turnover with those accounts, because a lot of people either didn't pay their bills or didn't continue with the service after the free trial was over.

It was the least costly way to get a new account, but when we started to do return-on-investment analysis, we realized it was also the least profitable, because these accounts had the lowest stay time.

To see it at work, I went on a ride with a route sales rep to one of the poorer neighborhoods in Long Beach, California, and in a number of these homes the water cooler was almost the only piece of furniture in the living room. When I walked in I thought right away, *How in the world are they paying for home delivery of bottled water?* Much as at Deer Park, I inherited a losing atmosphere that was demoralizing, and it sucked the life out of a lot of our people.

BYRON: MAGICAL MOTIVATION

When you put on that purple and gold, you have to have that winner mentality. That's just how it goes. It's how I feel, how all my teammates feel, and how every Lakers player felt up until recently, maybe.

Magic epitomized that winner's mentality. He brought out the best in everyone around him. He worked hard, played team basketball, and was a vocal yet caring leader. He would get on you, but then he'd give you a big old hug afterward and be your loudest cheerleader when you made an adjustment and used it in a game.

During the preseason before he retired, we were in Italy, but Magic was sick and didn't play. Then when we were back in the States we had a game in Utah and he was with the team.

We didn't know what he was dealing with yet, so we'd give him shit because our motto was when you put that uniform on, you better be ready to perform. No excuses. So on the bus to play Utah, we'd say, "Are you going to play, man? You took a couple of weeks off, are you ready to play?" Just giving him a hard time, because that's what we all did to each other.

"Yeah, I'm ready, I'm ready."

"All right, all right."

But he wasn't himself. He wasn't Magic.

When we went over to shoot around that morning he wasn't there. He had flown back to LA. He couldn't go.

But that was Magic; he was always ready until his body told him he couldn't do it anymore. He was a fighter and he was going to be on the bus with the team until he absolutely couldn't be there anymore.

He didn't look at his situation and give up. He didn't throw in the towel and settle for last place in life. Magic was a winner and he'd continue to make the people around him better no matter what he was doing.

That season Magic returned to play in the All-Star Game and put on the most inspirational and memorable all-star performance of all time. He scored twenty-five points, dished out nine assists, hit a three in the final seconds that will go down in history, and walked away MVP of the game.

That summer in the Olympics, he was a leader on the Dream Team and one of the faces of USA basketball shining on a world stage. Magic looked like the Magic of old as he helped the USA cruise to the gold medal. Afterward, in the 1992–93 season, when he came back briefly, we were destroying people. It was probably one of our weakest teams in my time there, but when Magic was on the court, anything was possible.

He's a winner, and when a winner steps on the court it brings out the winner in everyone around him. He does it now in business and in the community and in the gym, where Charlie and I work out alongside him all the time. He's never looked healthier, and his will to win has never been stronger.

CHARLIE: CHANGING THE MENTALITY

When I got to McKesson, our annual quit rate was nearly 60 percent, and something like 70 percent of all of our new customers came from the route sales reps' knocking on doors and offering those free trials. We had half a million customers, so we had to replace three hundred thousand of them every year just to break even. At least a hundred thousand of them were drinking water free for a couple of months and then not paying their bills.

When the team has a loser mentality, bad things happen. There are people who coast through their jobs and don't care about success, and there are people who will lie and cheat for their own benefit to collect a paycheck they haven't earned.

At McKesson Water there was an embarrassing moment for the company when a man we thought was one of our best route sales reps turned out to have made a career-ending mistake. We nominated him for the International Bottled Water Association Route Driver of the Year Award because he had been such a great leader and his numbers were through the roof. After the nomination we found out he had actually falsified his sales by emptying full bottles of water and returning the empties to the company. We, of course, had to rescind his nomination and fire a man we'd thought was one of our best employees.

But then, on the flip side, in times of need the strong come through. Our city faced a time of tragedy in 1994 when the Northridge earthquake devastated the San Fernando Valley area of Los Angeles. There were fifty-seven fatalities, and nearly nine thousand people injured from this natural disaster that caused more than $20 billion in damage.

I was flying to Arizona that day but flew home right away and joined the drivers on the routes, and we delivered more bottles that day than any other day of my career. In a time of need, when there was high volume to move, the team played like all-stars and certainly made me proud.

That was the case the majority of the time with the sales reps. When we cured the loser mentality that existed when I arrived at both water companies, the true colors of these sales reps shone through. Once we turned the company around at McKesson Water, the average route sales rep in southern California was making $60,000 per year, and the best ones were making over $100,000 annually. That's a solid wage for the 1990s.

More important, though, was the respect they earned with the customers. Whenever a route would get too large (mainly due to the success of the driver), we'd have to break it up and add additional sales reps. Our biggest concern about breaking up a route was that to those customers who knew their route sales rep, the water tasted better, the cooler was cleaner, the truck ran more smoothly—everything about the company was better because they had a direct relationship with the company through that route sales rep. When we gave them a new rep, that's when a customer would say, "Maybe I'm going to leave now."

That's how strong the relationship was between customer and rep. They would never leave when that route sales rep they knew was servicing them. That was a problem for us, but it was a good problem, because it meant our people were out there trying to win. It meant that they weren't just selling water; they were forging relationships and building a better brand for themselves and for the team. It was a winning mentality for a team that at one point had definitely lost its way.

X's and O's

- When changes are on the horizon, the work might be greater, but so is the reward.

- Once you think you can't win, you've already lost.

- Positive reinforcement from a leader is the most critical when times are tough.

- If you spend too much time dwelling on the past, your future will suffer.

Chapter 7

No Panic

"It ain't over 'til it's over." —*Yogi Berra*

The best leaders rise to the occasion when the chips are down. Success comes when everyone remains focused and fights to the very end.

BYRON: EIGHT POINTS IN NINE SECONDS

Sometimes winning comes easy. Actually, it's never easy, but when all things are clicking and the focus is there, winning might start to feel easy. But a true champion plays to the final whistle no matter what the situation. The season is never over and the game is never over until there are all zeros on the clock.

With that fight to push to the finish line that exists within a champion, there is also the mentality that under no circumstances do you panic. It's a mind-set that some are born with and others develop through experience. Once you've seen a miracle, you start to believe in miracles.

One of the more memorable games of my career came when I was in Indiana and Reggie Miller scored eight points in nine seconds against the Knicks. It's a game that's been celebrated often in the twenty years since it happened.

It was the 1995 Eastern Conference Semifinals, and we were facing a New York Knicks team who had beaten us in the Eastern Conference Finals the year before after we were up 3–2. That year they lost to the Houston Rockets in the Finals, so this time they were gunning for a championship. We were gunning for them. It was a true rivalry, and we even signed former Knick Mark Jackson to help give us that edge.

As on our Lakers teams, the players—Patrick Ewing, Anthony Mason, Charles Oakley, John Starks, and company—had that motivation to win it all because they had been so close. And as our Lakers teams had, they had Pat Riley as their coach.

Riles wanted to win every possession of every game. That's who he was. He wanted guys to fight and claw and do whatever it took to be champions. Even during the regular season, Riley preached winning by any means necessary. He didn't rest guys once we had the playoffs locked up, because there was always a better seed or a home court advantage to get. He didn't let anyone lose focus for even one play, because he knew more than anyone that anything could happen. He was a fight-to-the-death kind of coach, so even though his team was up 105–99 at home with 18.7 seconds, I knew more than anyone that his team wouldn't just relax.

We had the ball and Reggie immediately hit a three after getting the inbounds pass from Mark Jackson at half-court. Anthony Mason grabbed it for a quick inbound, but we had them pretty well covered. He tried to lob the ball to Greg Anthony, but I was in front and Reggie was in back and Greg tripped over his own feet and fell to the ground. I know Knicks fans like to tell a different story, but he just ran out of room and hit the deck.

Either way, it made it easy for Reggie to steal the inbounds pass, and when he did I jumped behind the three-point line, ready for the pass in the corner. Instead he had the awareness to take a step back and shoot it himself. Just like that it was tied at 105.

John Starks got fouled on the inbound play, but the pressure was too great, and he missed both free throws. The ball bounced around after the second miss, and Reggie got fouled after he finally grabbed the rebound with 7.5 seconds left. With ice in his veins he hit both foul shots and put us up 107–105 to give us game one in the series on the road.

CHARLIE: TRUST YOUR GUT

In business you can never panic. You have to believe that you are going to win until you are completely out of options. The second you give up, it's over. The second you as CEO see someone give up, it should be over for that person as well. A guy who shows up to work, goes through the motions, and collects his paycheck is never going to hit the big shot for the company.

When you're investing you have to have the same mentality. At this stage of my career I tend to invest in businesses that have a certain size, have proven out their concept in the market, and have positive cash flow. I sit on the board of a number of companies and have investments in many businesses where that investment plan is in place. But an opportunity to invest in a start-up came my way, and I knew that with the right team, we could walk away winners.

The company was called Freshpet, and it landed in my lap in an interesting way. Nestlé, my former employer, bought Ralston Purina, and as a condition from the government for the sale to go through it had to spin off Meow Mix, a Ralston Purina brand. It became an independent company that was acquired by a private equity firm.

That firm sold it to a second private equity firm that was about to sell it to Del Monte, but several of the Meow Mix senior managers didn't want to work for a large company again. In anticipation of this sale they developed a manufacturing process to make all-natural refrigerated pet food, and they were testing it in twelve stores in the Bay Area when I got a phone call from Dick Kassar, CFO of Meow Mix.

"There are three of us testing this," he said. "I think it would be a great business opportunity, if you're interested."

They were looking to raise $7 million, and I told management that I would get the funds. At the eleventh hour, an Australian company that was selling refrigerated pet food in its home country decided it wanted to put the money up itself, so Dick said to me, "Since you've done all this work, I'll let you invest one million dollars if you're interested, and you'll be a passive investor."

I put up half and a person I partner with on a lot of businesses put up half, and we were passive investors while they were doing this test. Five months went by and I got a phone call from Dick.

"Del Monte is going to buy Meow Mix," he said. "We have an opportunity to hire all the best Meow Mix people, and we want to build a factory."

The decision was now in my hands. He was willing to give me a 40 percent return on my original investment and I could walk away a winner, or I could roll the dice and re-up on my investment.

This was the business version of me with the ball in my hands and a game-winning shot to take. Except in this case to stay in the game I needed to raise $25 million ($14 million of equity, $11 million of preferred debt) to match the $14 million of equity capital the management team was putting in from the sale of Meow Mix, and raise the additional funds needed for working capital. If I did that, each group would own 50 percent of the company.

BYRON: COACHING WITH OPTIMISM

While it was an exciting moment, obviously, it was also a good lesson in not giving up. For Reggie to hit those shots and win the game, the whole team needed to have the mind-set that we still had a chance. We were down six with 18.7 seconds left, and I'm sure a lot of Pacers fans turned their TVs off, but the players didn't have that mentality.

There was still time on the clock, and that's how everybody on the team looked at it—and they had to, because negativity is contagious. If one of the five guys on the court thinks it's over, then it's over. If Coach Larry Brown thinks it's over, then it's over. Everyone needs to be on the same page.

Coach Brown was always the optimist. He is a mentor for me in a number of ways, but what stood out the most was how much he loved the players and how much he believed in us, both on and off the court. With that first inbounds pass, the play he set up had me curling around a screen first and then Reggie following behind. Either of us could get the ball and take the shot, and in general he believed that anyone on the team had the ability to hit the big shot when called upon.

As the head coach you're the general of the team, and if the players see you panic, then they're going to panic. There was no panic in the eyes of Larry Brown in that game, and when I was a head coach I had that same Larry Brown mentality.

When I was coaching the then–New Jersey Nets, we blew a big lead and lost an important playoff game to the Boston Celtics. We were on the road, but we were up by a lot and should have walked away with the win. Instead of being up in the series 2–1, we were down 2–1. After the game all the reporters were asking about how devastating it was and asking how we could possibly bounce back from a loss like this. But it didn't faze me.

The next day I almost overslept for a meeting. That's how well I slept. I wasn't worried. I knew the kind of team we had. I knew we were better.

I walked in the next day and said, "Hey, we're in great shape, we came here to win one game, and we can still do that." The veteran guys on the team were with me, but my tone and my demeanor really helped our younger guys at the time like Kenyon Martin, Kerry Kittles, and Richard Jefferson. As a coach you're always really talking to the young guys in the room—especially when it comes to confidence building—and I wanted to really make sure that they understood I wasn't panicking.

I set the tone by acknowledging that we'd lost the game, and then I went over the tape, showing how we'd lost the big lead and making the corrections so it wouldn't happen again. "Let's play with the same intensity for forty-eight minutes and close it out." That was my message to our guys. When the leader comes in and shows that type of confidence in his troops, they're going to feed off that. If they see an ounce of worry on the face of the coach, it's over. Some coaches can fake it, but that's not my style. I'm naturally confident and I'm really not going to panic in those situations.

You can do that when you've assembled the right team and know that they're capable of being champions. Larry Brown knew that about us in Indiana, and I knew it about my guys in New Jersey. We came back and won the series against the Celtics and went to the NBA Finals, and honestly, there was never a doubt in my mind that we would do so.

CHARLIE: FIGHTING THROUGH DOUBT

I want to project the same positive attitude that Byron does, but internally I'm not always as tough. It's really important that your people feel that as the leader you're still genuinely enthusiastic and truly believe that the mission is doable. Even when there are bumps along the way, you've got to project that the team is going to win this fight. As soon as you start projecting doubt, you put a seed of doubt in the minds of your people that can really devastate morale. If they feel that I no longer believe in what we're trying to get accomplished, they'll give up on reaching their goals.

I keep a brave face, but there have definitely been times when I went home at night and tossed and turned, fretting over whether or not we'd be able to achieve our goals. But I'm always able to lift myself out of that in front of my organization.

I was genuinely concerned when I was running the McKesson Water Products Company and doing the reorganization while the California economy tanked. The housing market crashed, jobs were down, and many Americans were feeling the effects of a recession.

When the California economy tanked, one of the things that people could do without was a water cooler at home. They could go to the store and buy water if they had to, or sacrifice the benefits of bottled water and drink from the tap.

Due to this collapse we were losing customers at the same time that our reorganization was taking place and affecting our customer base. It wasn't something I could have predicted, and the timing was terrible. It certainly put doubts in my head that we'd be able to turn the company around quickly enough that I'd be able to keep my job, but I never second-guessed the reorganization.

The team, of course, certainly had doubts. There were misunderstandings among the employee group, one of which was that on paper we were showing that we were generating a lot of cash, when actually we were not generating a lot of free cash at the end of the day because we were so capital intensive. We were using virtually all the cash we were generating to buy more route trucks, to buy more water coolers, and to catch up on maintenance because my predecessor had not been spending the money necessary to keep the fleet in good shape, keep the uniforms looking pristine, and purchase the required production lines.

So in a time when we were losing customers, I was forced to spend to keep the company moving in the right direction. If that doesn't make you sweat, nothing will.

To help people understand, I had to go out and explain the mechanics of cash flow to each of the 56 branches and plants in our organization. I felt that it was really important to do this myself and send the right message. Everyone in the company owned stock in McKesson Co., so everyone would benefit if the water division did well, because it would ultimately affect the stock price of the company. So I went armed with a chalkboard or a flip chart and showed how the cash was accounted for through profit-and-loss statements. I would go out and talk about the various ways we could increase earnings, and where depreciation and amortization came into play. I showed that we were using our earnings to buy more route trucks, water coolers, and equipment for the plants. It was a real eye-opener for people.

Over time, I'd say a good percentage got it. Some people never got it and never understood that even though we were saying we were making $25 million before interest, taxes, depreciation, and amortization, it wasn't real because we had to spend so much to keep the company going forward and growing.

When times are the toughest, it's on the leader to rally the team and keep confidence high. Even if I'm losing sleep, I have to go door-to-door with a smile on my face and explain to every person why I still believe. When you are the most concerned is when you need to exude the most confidence. In this case it kept the team moving forward, and in the end we won.

BYRON: BELIEVING IN YOUR TEAMMATES

The coach may be the first line of defense against pushing the panic button, but the players have to believe too. In the Pacers-Knicks game, if I'd just given up and stood there after Reggie Miller hit the first shot, Greg Anthony would have been open and might not have fallen, and the outcome would've been different. Once Reggie got the ball again, if I hadn't gotten to my spot, my defender could have easily gone to help on Reggie and all of a sudden he wouldn't have the open shot.

You could look over the court and say the same for every player on our team. That winning mentality played just as big a role in winning that game as anything that happened on the court. And you don't have to even touch the ball to make the difference.

To win at anything you have to give maximum effort, and you must have that never-say-die, never-give-up mentality until the clock is at 0.0 in order to perform at your best. So what's going on in your head is just as important as what you're doing with your hands and feet.

Of course, in this particular game, there was no one who wanted us to panic more than Spike Lee, who was sitting courtside and taunting Reggie the entire game. That just added motivation for a guy like Reggie, who is a Hall of Famer and one of the greatest two-guards to play the sport.

After every shot he would look Spike dead in the eye, and Spike would stand up and bark back. When John Starks missed those free throws, Reggie gave Spike a choke sign, and it was lights out. Reggie,

Larry Bird, Michael Jordan, Magic Johnson—those are guys you just don't keep talking trash to, because they use it to fuel their fire.

What's funny is that the fans and the New York media like to blame Spike for the Knicks' losing that game, as if Reggie hit those shots (or Starks missed his free throws) because of him. It may have riled Reggie up, but it's not like Spike was out there playing defense. He didn't have anything to do with the outcome. At best he was a fun distraction. What really won us that game, and eventually the series, was our ability to play to the best of our ability until the very end. There was no panic. There was no quitting. There were 18.7 seconds left on the clock, and, as it turned out, that was 7.5 seconds more than we needed.

CHARLIE: GETTING PEOPLE ON BOARD

When you choose the tougher path in any financial situation, you have to fight the natural instinct to panic. I could have taken the easy money and called it a day, but when you're going for the big win, you'll always be tested.

I needed to raise $25 million to stay in the game, and there's pressure that comes along with that. When you present an opportunity to people, you want them to walk away winners if they choose to join the team. Nothing is guaranteed in life, but I was selling them on Freshpet based on my own confidence in the company, and I didn't want to be wrong.

You could panic in that situation, but if you did you'd never find the strength to be successful in any investing opportunity. Instead I turned to Ric Kayne, founder of Kayne Anderson Capital Advisors, who had split the initial $1 million investment with me, and formulated a plan to create an investment team.

Ric and I had invested together in both Glacier Water and Day Runner, and in both instances I'd become chairman of the board and brought in new CEOs to run the business. He was confident that I had a good sense of how to run a business and how to evaluate executives. Both of those investments had had good outcomes, so he was confident we could deliver.

Together he and I put in more of our own money, and then we held two meetings with potential investors to gauge interest. We brought out the management team from Freshpet to present the Freshpet story. It was a sales pitch, but it also let this group hear the very real confidence and enthusiasm the team had about the company. By the end we had commitments of $32 million from a group of about thirty-five people, when we'd needed to raise only $25 million.

Going into the meetings, we hadn't been sure what the response would be. We wanted enough people in the room that we would get the $25 million. Some people in this group were friends of mine or past investment partners, but the majority were investors with Ric, and his endorsement was enough to seal the deal. Ric also invited a number of his managers to sit in on the presentation, and by the end the managers wanted in too.

We could have just taken more money from fewer people, but because we are both loyal to our friends and business partners, we wanted to give everyone a small investment in the company. It was actually more complicated for us because we had to manage that many more people, but it was worth it.

Confidence is the kryptonite for panic. When you have a group that believes in you, and you believe in the company, there is never a reason to panic. A couple of years later we needed $7 million more, and City National Bank, which had a great relationship with Ric and me because of Glacier Water, loaned the money to Freshpet.

A few years after that we needed to raise $60 million to take the company to the next level, and we didn't want to bring in another private equity firm or other major investor. That would have seriously diluted the ownership position of the management team and made for some very unhappy people running the business.

Instead we worked with three primary banks, including City National again, and got creative by having the investors guarantee the loans in order for the banks to get on board. They didn't have to put up any money, but whatever their guarantee was, they had to have that amount of money available in a liquid state, which was a very unusual arrangement. We got the investors to agree to do that because they were given an interest rate that was converted into stock.

I convinced them to do it by explaining how the returns on that guarantee would more than justify the annoyance of having to keep the money in a liquid form as a condition of the bank loan. With the personal guarantees, the loan got approved, and everyone was incredulous that I'd gotten the deal done. Ric and I may have broken a sweat, but we never panicked, because we knew that the business was good and it was about to get better.

X's and O's

- The opportunity for success is not over until you've exhausted all options.

- True champions never stop trying to win.

- When a leader remains confident and optimistic, the rest of the team will follow his or her lead.

- The only way to remove doubt is to clearly explain the plan for future success.

Chapter 8

Risk

"You cannot swim for new horizons until you have courage to lose sight of the shore." —*William Faulkner*

Confidence plays a huge role in the success of a leader. You have to believe not only in yourself and your ability to be great, but also that the support around you will come through when called upon.

BYRON: BETTING ON YOURSELF

After two seasons with the Indiana Pacers and one with the expansion Vancouver Grizzlies, I knew my NBA career was likely coming to a close.

In a perfect world I would retire a Laker. That was the dream at the time, and as it turned out, GM Jerry West was there to help make my dream come true.

The team had just traded for Kobe Bryant and got Shaquille O'Neal through free agency, so it was at the start of something great before the 1996–97 season, when Jerry told me he had a spot for me.

"We're going to need your leadership," he said, "but you're going to have to make the team. It won't be a guaranteed contract."

Now, there are a number of ways a person can react to that statement. The initial instinct might be to let pride take over and whine and scream about what I'd done for the organization. How dare they make me earn a spot on the roster? Didn't three rings in ten seasons do that?

But that's not who I am. That's not a champion's mentality. I played every game with something to prove, so to me this was nothing. I was happy to have the opportunity, and I was confident in my ability to do what it took to make the team.

Was it risky to reach for the stars and sign with the Lakers when I likely could have walked right onto a lesser team? Sure. But it was worth it to me to finish my career in purple and gold.

Once I put my name on that piece of paper, I knew I'd make it. Even though it wasn't a guaranteed contract, to me it was a guarantee.

When I played really well during the first few days of training camp, Jerry came to talk to me.

"Young man," he said, "you're doing well. You keep playing like this, and you're going to make the team."

I just kind of smiled. I knew I was making the team. He was just keeping me on my toes and making sure this old man didn't coast through training camp.

Once it was official and I did make the team, I felt the same excitement as the first time I'd put on the jersey. When you love the game, you appreciate every opportunity. Being a Laker was special, and I knew that this was probably my last shot at playing for the team I loved.

On the other end of the bench that year was Kobe Bryant, who was probably the most reserved eighteen-year-old I had ever seen.

He was real into ball—lived, ate, slept basketball—but he was quiet and reserved. The first time I met him was at a rookie transitional program, and for the whole week he called me Mr. Scott. I said, "Look, you can call me Byron," and he responded, "OK, Mr. Scott." That's just the kind of kid he was. He respected the game and he appreciated putting on the jersey as much as I did.

Kobe was so focused. He didn't care about having friends or doing anything outside of basketball. One day in the back of the team bus, I sat down with him and talked to him about his goals.

"What do you want to be in this league?" I asked. "What do you want to accomplish?"

He paused for maybe two seconds, and said, "I want to be the best player in this league."

At that time he was coming in at eight thirty in the morning, shooting in the Forum when the lights were still off. I would go back there to get treatment for my ailing body parts and everything, and he would be out there by himself. He had the will and the determination, but he wasn't getting much playing time that first year. When he told me that, I said, "You will be. You keep working the way you work and you will be."

Kobe was full of confidence, but that doesn't always translate on the court. Some guys get out there and crumble the second it gets hard. That was never going to happen to a guy like Kobe Bryant, but it was my job that year to encourage him to take risks and push him to achieve his goal.

CHARLIE: BETTING ON THE JOCKEY

A big part of risk is trust. Byron had to trust himself that he could make the team, but the coaches and team had to trust in him as a leader too. They had to know that his value was great and understand what he brought to the table.

When I first got involved with Freshpet, it was Dick Kassar, then CFO of Meow Mix, who reached out with the offer. I knew Dick from summering in Vermont. I played bridge with him. He was a sharp businessman, but also an all-around good person. I do business only with people like that. I need to know someone first. I bet on the jockey, not the horse. I have to be confident that the person I'm investing in is really good at what he or she does. It's how I make decisions. For Dick it was the same thing. He likes to compare me to Larry David from *Curb Your Enthusiasm* and jokes that every one of my stories "starts with Adam and Eve." We knew we were great partners in bridge, and we knew we'd be great partners on this project.

When you are stepping outside your comfort zone with investing, you limit your risk by fully believing in the people you're working with. A 40 percent return on my original investment after just five months was great money, but I trusted that sticking with Dick and raising the funds would lead to something even better. It was a risk, and there was a lot of money at stake, but I liked the management team and believed in the concept.

Freshpet was a start-up but was unique in the amount of difficulties a competitor would have entering the market. In every supermarket or pet store we entered, we owned the refrigerator and essentially the real estate within the store. A second company would have real trouble getting a second refrigerator in, and wouldn't be able to put product in our fridge because we owned it. That command of the real estate, along with the trend of the humanization of pets (people spending more money to feed their animals better than humans), made Freshpet feel like a winner even though it was a company starting from scratch. So while I was shifting away from my normal investing plan, it was a calculated risk.

Just as I put my trust in Dick Kassar, the banks had to put their trust in me. In the case of the City National Bank, the executive vice president of specialty banking, Bob Iritani, is someone who also bets on the jockey, not the horse. City National had funded Glacier Water, so it knew that I always did what I said I was going to do, and that if things were going wrong, I told the bank, so there were never any surprises.

While Bob cared about Freshpet and the barriers to entry and everything I thought would make it successful, the fact that I was the one who thought it was going to be successful was what sold him on giving us the loan. When I approached him about it, he trusted me and thought we could get it done, because of the success of the deal we'd made for Glacier Water Vending.

So it became this circle of trust among the bank, me, and the investors, and with Dick Kassar that made the risk seem like less of a risk. Byron knew the Lakers organization, he trusted Jerry West, who was always honest with him, and he could look at guys like Kobe and Shaq and know it was going to be a successful venture. Just as I could have walked away early and made 40 percent on my investment, he could have signed with another franchise and not worried about making the team, but when there is a solid circle of trust, you stop thinking about the risk and start focusing on the reward.

BYRON: REINING IN RISK

As a coach you always want to encourage risk. When I was an assistant coach with the Sacramento Kings, the captain of the risk takers, Jason Williams, was one of the stars of the team. White Chocolate—who by the way hated that nickname—was an amazing talent. He would do things that were so spectacular that your jaw would just drop to the floor. But there were times when he was frustrating from a coach's standpoint, because he would come down and play a showboat style of playground basketball.

There's a difference between a wild roll of the dice and a calculated risk. In basketball we teach calculated risks. Never fear the big shot, but make it only when it's the right play.

In his first few years J-Will never took into consideration the clock, the score, or the situation. He just played, which at times frustrated both his teammates and head coach Rick Adelman. But for the most part the kid played with the right attitude. He wanted to win, and he wanted to play for his teammates, but he didn't always know how to properly play the odds, because he had been playing this style of basketball all his life.

As his coach I tried to put the brakes on his wild style of play as often as possible. He would do something crazy and during a timeout I'd say, "J, just a nice little chest pass, you don't have to go around your back and try and hit it with your elbow."

"I hear you, Coach, I hear you."

What he meant was, *I hear you, but leave me alone.*

He had that type of attitude, but I loved him because he was fun to be around and he had no agenda. He just wanted to play and enjoy the game. He wasn't worried about money or playing time, and there was no ego there. You don't get a lot of guys like that— guys who just love the game of basketball.

A lot of times guys let all the other stuff get in the way, and then the purest form of the game kind of escapes them. Jason, he had that pure form all the time. But he would just drive me crazy because there would be two minutes left in a game, and we'd have a six-point lead, and he'd take a quick shot that we didn't need. We could try for that shot twenty seconds later, with less time on the shot clock. If you left him open, Jason was going to shoot it. He didn't play the odds.

With someone like Jason, experience was key. As he matured with the Kings, and then when he moved on to the Memphis Grizzlies and Miami Heat, he grew into a player who learned when to hold 'em and when to fold 'em.

Experience and knowledge of the game helped him improve more than someone like me sitting him down and telling him what to do. Like everyone, he wanted to win, so when he was ready to take it upon himself to make changes in order to win, he did just that. He was still taking risks with his shots and passes, but they were calculated risks, and in 2006 with the Miami Heat he went all in and won a championship.

CHARLIE: DON'T GO ALL IN ON A LOSING HAND

Trust and risk go hand in hand on many levels. Whether it's with a rookie or a seasoned veteran, you have to trust people to not only take the shot, but also recover if they miss. Anytime I have someone working for me in any capacity I want to encourage them to take risks, but I have to be able to trust them first.

When assigning projects to key managers I'll focus on the strategy for what we're trying to accomplish, and ask them to come back with tactics. Once we've agreed on the tactics, I let them do it. If they make mistakes, I let them tell me how they're going to correct things. The more you can let people learn from their own mistakes, the better off they're going to be long-term and the better off the company will ultimately be. That person will be more comfortable taking risks, and it's really important that people be willing to take risks without feeling as if they'll be punished if they're not successful. As long as they don't make the same error twice, then it's OK.

I think communicating with both the people you're reporting to and the people reporting to you is important. I don't like to be surprised, and I don't like for others to be surprised. When I was working my way up to the CEO level, I never felt any shame in going to a superior and discussing something that was going wrong. We'd talk about it and we'd adjust. I've always had that mind-set, and I never felt I would be punished for asking for help when I needed it. As a CEO I tried to lead in the same way.

When you don't trust someone enough to have that relationship and let him or her take risks, you shouldn't get into business with that person in the first place. When I was with McKesson we were looking to expand the Sparkletts brand to Seattle, and I ran into a situation where trust became a problem.

The easiest way to expand in a city is to buy another company. What we had successfully done in most cities was buy a company and use that as a foundation from which to expand. In Seattle I knew the person who ran the largest bottled water company, so we negotiated with this person, and we thought we had a deal.

It was a family-owned business and his dad and his brother were also involved. They were each one-third partners. This guy wanted us to cut a special deal that gave him more than a third of the profits from the sale of the company. I told him right away that we weren't going to do anything under the table. We'd give him the price he wanted, but it would all be aboveboard, and however ownership was shared among the three of them, that's how the payout would be structured.

Ultimately the negotiation broke down because we wouldn't meet his demands. I came away from that episode angry that the guy was so duplicitous that he'd want to cheat his own family. I knew I couldn't trust him, and I'm not going to take a risk on someone I don't trust.

If we had bought his company, we would also have wanted him to run the Seattle territory. We were going to invest a lot of money in the region, so he could have made a lot more. But once I knew I couldn't trust him, I didn't have the foundation to go forward with his company.

Family dynamics is a very complex subject. It's easy to say you want somebody who's a great family man, but what's more important to me is that I want somebody who is honest, and is going to work hard and care about what he does. Personal family issues aside, I want somebody who is a great business partner to go to war with.

When the deal didn't work out, we needed a new plan. I talked to my head of route operations at Sparkletts and we decided that we loved this market, so we would get in it ourselves from scratch. So we went and we got a branch location. We moved people from other parts of the country, and we started to sell Sparkletts in the market against this person who wanted to cheat his family members out of money. It was costly and a risk, but not as big a risk as getting into business with the wrong people. It took quite a while, but we ended up being the largest home and office water delivery company in the Pacific Northwest. The other guy had to settle for second place.

BYRON: NEVER LET A SMALL FAILURE DEFINE FUTURE SUCCESS

Kobe was different. He was a student of the game who, from day one, was a sponge. He wanted to hear everything I had to say. He wanted to hear what everyone had to say, and he was never afraid to ask questions. Both he and point guard Derek Fisher would ask about the Lakers championships and what we'd done to win. They were both big into eighties basketball then and they would listen to stories with childlike enthusiasm. They loved Showtime, and Kobe was always saying, "I wish I was playing back then." My response was always, "Well, I'm glad you weren't, because I would've been coming off the bench."

That rookie year, though, it was the other way around. He was eighteen and I was thirty-six, but at the time he wasn't even sixth man. We had Eddie Jones and Nick Van Exel, so Kobe didn't play a whole hell of a lot.

But he was a fighter. I knew he was special right away. In the gym he worked harder than anyone else. On the court he was a pit bull— just aggressive every chance he got. You need players who have that mentality. Kobe has that mentality, that killer instinct. He wants to win, and he'll do whatever it takes to win.

In the second round of the playoffs he got his chance to shine. We were playing the Utah Jazz, and in game four I sprained my wrist pretty bad. I was playing a lot in the playoffs, so it shook up the lineup when I went in the locker room and didn't go back in the game.

The next day my wrist swelled up as we were flying to Utah. I went out before the game to see if I could shoot, and I couldn't reach the basket from six feet. I told Del Harris, who was the coach at the time, that I couldn't go. That moved Kobe up.

In game five—which was an elimination game for us—he was put in the position in the last couple of minutes of the game to take big shots. Instead of coming through, however, he threw up three air balls between the fourth quarter and overtime. After each one the Utah fans screamed, "Aaaaair ballll" louder and louder. It was tough to watch.

That day I said to Del, "I'm telling you, that kid, I know him. He's going to come back even stronger because of that." I wasn't around the next year, but in Kobe's second season, he was the leading bench scorer in the league and he made the all-star team. Then, of course, you know how the rest worked out for him: eighteen all-star appearances, five championships, an MVP award, and just a whole houseful of trophies.

Not letting those shots affect you is in your DNA when you are a winner. It's part of who you are. First of all, you've got to have enough guts to take the shots in the first place. You have to be willing to fail. He hadn't played much all year, but he came in and took those shots as if he'd been playing all season long.

He was willing to give his all—at eighteen years old—and that's why I knew he was going be great. We had some veterans on the floor who did not want to take the shots that Kobe took. Not being blamed for a loss was more important to them than potentially being responsible for a victory. That's not a champion's mind-set. Winners want that opportunity and Kobe never shied away from having the ball in his hands. Even after he put up two air balls, he didn't mind. He went out there and shot a third. He was willing to be the goat just as much as he yearned to be the hero.

Until his last game day he trusted himself more than he trusted anybody else on the floor. Most great players are like that. To earn their trust, you have to show them that you're not going to back down, you're not scared to take the big shots. Then they'll have that trust in you.

Magic was built differently. Magic would take the shot, but he was more than willing to make the pass to the open player for the right shot. He wasn't thinking about whether the other person was going to make the shot or not. He was just thinking about the right basketball play to make. It's a different mentality, but I think they both ended up doing OK.

CHARLIE: THE POKER FACE

You have to be flexible in your decisions. You have to be willing to move from one option to another based on circumstances. You have to be willing to take risks. And you have to do it with as little emotion as possible. Byron never shows his emotions. He believes in himself the way Kobe believes in himself, and he believes in his guys the way Magic does, so even when times are tough, he stands strong. When we get together for a game of liar's poker, it's an incredible challenge figuring him out. That poker face is key in taking risks. If your team sees you sweat, they start to sweat.

At Freshpet we were dealt a number of blows early on, and I too needed to stand strong and power forward. The trends were great for Freshpet, but right at the time we started this company, the economy tanked. It was not good timing for launching a new high-end product. We'd thought we could just go in and sell the idea and have no problem getting accounts to understand it, but we were met with a lot of pushback.

We were trying to change how people bought pet food. We provided the refrigerators, and they required a total reorganization of the planogram—the layout of product placement displayed in a store—in an aisle that had no electricity.

You had to bring electricity to the pet food aisle, and it was not an easy sell. We went through that $39 million (the equity plus the working capital) a whole lot faster than we'd expected, and growth was much slower. We were adding maybe a thousand stores a year, but we were piling up operating losses in a big way. That was partly because the economy was bad, and partly because even though the concept was great, and senior management of the various retail outlets really got it, their field people found it extremely difficult. They were not thrilled about it. They didn't want to have to go through all this work installing electrical and doing an entire planogram reorganization just for our product.

We were off to a bad start. Some people might start second-guessing their decision at this point, but a winner focuses on what he can do to win, not what he should have done to avoid a loss.

Over the years I've learned that there are small victories within every failure, including the reward of simply having taken the risk in the first place. Throughout my career I've come to realize that you don't want to chop someone's head off for taking a risk; instead you want to encourage it. At Freshpet there was a lot of risk, and the management team was trailblazing with an all-natural refrigerated product, so they were going to make mistakes along the way, and I had to allow people to do that. If they failed from time to time, and learned from their mistakes, then they were better prepared the next time. Failure isn't just a stepping-stone, it's a milestone on the road to future success.

X's and O's

- Your résumé never speaks for itself, so continue to prove yourself throughout your career.

- True leaders grow from their willingness to take risks, regardless of the outcome.

- Be honest about successes and failures, and when there is failure, explain what you have learned and how you will fix it.

- Show your team members that you trust them. If you don't trust them, make changes.

Chapter 9

Success Outside Your Element

"The purpose of life is to live it, to taste experience to the utmost, to reach out eagerly and without fear for newer and richer experience."
—Eleanor Roosevelt

When you step out of your comfort zone to play a new kind of game, the rules may change, but a champion adapts and brings his or her knowledge and ability to the table in order to find victory.

BYRON: ADAPTING TO A NEW ENVIRONMENT

After that last season with the Lakers I felt satisfied with my NBA career. I spent eleven out of fourteen seasons in the league with the Lakers and won three championships, so I didn't need one more year with a new NBA team to prove anything to myself or anyone else. What I wanted was a bit of an adventure, so I looked into playing overseas.

My ex-wife's father was in the army, so she had been all over the place. When the idea of playing one more season out of the country came up, she liked the idea of going to Greece.

In the summer after the 1996–97 season, I signed with Panathinaikos of the Greek Basketball League, and it was a culture shock to say the least. Off the court, my family and I were living completely out of our element. My daughter and my younger son went to school with the kids from the US embassy, and after a couple of months my daughter was able to talk to the cashiers at the grocery store in Greek. It was pretty amazing!

For me the language barrier was a bit tougher. I had no clue what the locals were saying most of the time. Luckily our coach and assistant coach both spoke English very well, but when the head coach started talking about strategies he would always talk in Greek. The assistant would always be the interpreter, but it changes your approach mentally when you are looking for help from an assistant just to understand the play.

In the United States everything just came naturally. With Riley or Larry Brown, I almost knew what he was going to say before he said it. Here I didn't know what was going on at first. When you're out of your element it's like being a rookie all over again.

Each team in the Greek League was allowed to have two foreign-born players, so on my team it was me and Dino Radja, who had played in the NBA for the Celtics. Everyone on the team wanted to win, but Dino and I expected to win. The team hadn't won a championship in fourteen years, and we were brought in to change that. From day one, that was the goal.

My time in the locker room that season was probably the only time that I felt I couldn't really be myself as a leader, because my teammates didn't understand me most of the time. On the court, basketball is a universal language and your eyes and expressions and motions can say it all. When you put those hands out, all around the world they know that means, "Give me the ball." But because of the language barrier, I had to be more demonstrative on the floor and give my teammates the right looks to really get them to play hard. There were a whole lot of sign language and body language. When I couldn't express myself with my mouth, I had to talk with my actions.

Because of this, my on-court body language was all the more important. Since I couldn't really talk to the guys, they watched my every emotion even more carefully. If I looked upset or defeated in any way, the players would read that. Since they couldn't talk to me and get to know me personally, that was all they really had to go by.

As a player or a coach, I've always had the mentality that nothing was going to bother me. That turnover, that bad call—it's not going to bother me, because once a player sees me throwing a tantrum, then he feels that he has the right to do the same thing. Anger is contagious, and it doesn't lead to victory.

In order to win, everyone on the team has to be calm and collected and worried only about the next play, not a past play. When you can't speak English it's even more of a priority. To win you have to be on the same page, and if the book is written in a foreign language, you have to speak through emotions. Sometimes the best way to lead is with a glare and a smile.

CHARLIE: OLD KNOWLEDGE IN NEW PLACES

At Freshpet I was venturing down a road I hadn't been down before. Being the chairman of the board of a start-up company was something new for me at age sixty, but as with Byron, my will to win and the skill set that had made it work in the past were still the same.

One of the early difficulties was getting the refrigerator into the pet food aisle and the tremendous amount of work required to run electrical to an aisle that hadn't had electricity before. While that was a new problem, I was able to immediately draw comparisons to the water industry, where we'd had to pay for the water cooler, buy route trucks, put in more manufacturing lines, and spend money to make money.

I understood the cost of buying all these refrigerators. I knew the difficulty of getting a store to want to put a refrigerator in, because it was very much like getting a store to put in a vending machine for water. It's a very difficult sale. But I was also very familiar with the benefit of owning that refrigerator, because once it was in the store it was our real estate for as long as we wanted it.

The key to getting new customers is that you've got to go fishing when the fish are biting. There was a period in the evolution of the bottled water industry when it was the real poster child for growth. Sugar and soft drinks were the bad guys and water was the good guy because it was all natural with no calories. During its height, bottled water was the fastest-growing beverage category, so sales outweighed expenses, and getting the vending machines in stores and coolers in homes and offices became an easy sell.

This time the pet industry was similar. The pet food aisle was the fastest-growing aisle in the grocery category. The whole trend of the humanization of pets was something that I thought would have a long shelf life, so I saw this as being a fabulous opportunity, and it was really only a matter of time before it would click.

Yes, there were setbacks. The stock market crash hurt the growth rate of Freshpet because it raised doubts from the retailers that we would be able to continue to raise funds to survive. We were selling a premium product, and in general such products take a hit when the economy is in trouble.

When that happens, you have to be honest with your investors and remain calm. Our fundamentals of the business were still strong. The barrier to entry of number two, the fact that we'd never lost customers, and the continued growth (albeit at a slower rate) were all still reasons to stay the course. Fear and losing confidence in management are the main reasons people don't stay the course, so when stock is dropping, you can't run away from it. You have to be honest with yourself and your team about what's driving the plummeting stock, attack it head-on and prove that the company hasn't changed. It's still a strong company. The growing trend of feeding pets like humans was not changing, and there wasn't another competitor coming with a better mousetrap. We were still growing at 20 percent a year, even though we had said we were going to grow at 30 percent. Wall Street considers something that's growing at 5 percent a year a fast-growing company, so we were still in very good shape.

In the end, using the skills and knowledge that we'd had all along, we were able to make Freshpet a success, even though I was working outside my comfort zone. It was a new environment, but when you play your game, you can walk away a winner in any arena.

BYRON: UNFAMILIAR TERRITORY

Everything is different about playing overseas. The rules are different: the ball is live on the rim, so when you shoot a free throw and it bounces around, you can slap it off. That was one of the rules that I didn't get used to. When you play your whole life one way, it's hard to adjust to a different way. The key was also shaped differently. It was wider, to open up the game. And the three-point line was closer, which didn't make things easier for someone who'd spent his whole life in a rhythm from a certain distance.

The facilities were also very different. The top-notch gyms and

practice facilities we had in the NBA and the all-around accommo-
dations were head and shoulders above what the Greek League had
to offer. It didn't have the funds to create the environment that the
NBA did night in and night out either. All I cared about was winning, so that wasn't too much of an issue for me.

The biggest difference, though, was the fans. They were crazy. I
had never seen fans like that. The first road trip we took was to play
P.A.O.K., a team led by a young kid named Peja Stojakovic. That
was the first time I was ever frightened on a basketball court. The
fans in the stands were burning flags, giving us the finger, spitting at
us when we were on the court, and throwing drachmas, which are
about the size of a quarter.

They had little BIC lighters they would use to burn the coins before
throwing them on the court. The bench had Plexiglas over it, and at
first I wondered why, but I found out real quickly. We would just hear
all these coins hit the Plexiglas while we were sitting on the bench.

I went to get the ball one time after it rolled off the court, and one
of my teammates grabbed me. "No, no, no, no," he said. "Don't go
get that ball. They will start spitting on you."

"Really?" I couldn't believe it, but he was right.

It's tough to remain focused when all these things are going on
around you. If you're thinking about getting hit with loose change,
you're not exactly going to play your best basketball. Needless to say,
I played my worst game that first night. I think I had six points.

I just wanted to get the hell out of there. At one point somebody
threw a lead pipe on the floor. This wasn't basketball; this was ridiculous!
I'd never witnessed anything like that. On the way to the locker room a
coin hit me right in the head. I was literally afraid for my life. Everyone
else seemed to be used to it. After years in the NBA, this was not what I
was used to, and it was standing in the way of my performance.

CHARLIE: UNDERSTANDING DIFFERENT CULTURES

When you're out of your element you are prone to mistakes. When I was at Nestlé and going to various countries, I spent a month in Malaysia determining how best to introduce textured soy protein into the local cuisine. I was there with a Swiss experimental chef who worked in the research labs at Nestlé, and who was a true food connoisseur. The two of us were invited to dinner by the most important food broker Nestlé had in Malaysia. It was a dinner to die for—fifteen different dishes, one after the other, everyone drinking Johnnie Walker Black Label Scotch. Anytime we took a sip, the waiters were there refilling our glasses. I'm not a big Scotch drinker to begin with, but everyone was making toasts and having a good time, and the liquor flowed.

At the end of the evening, in an attempt to be funny and clever (and when I was a bit under the influence of alcohol), I said, "This meal was fabulous, but where were the spareribs?"

To me it was a joke, but they took it seriously. The room went silent.

"We're picking you up at eight tomorrow morning to take you for spareribs for breakfast," the broker said, breaking the silence.

I was the most senior person from Nestlé at the table, representing Nestlé Swiss headquarters, and in a matter of seconds I completely embarrassed the company and myself by insulting the hosts.

I was just making a joke, but it was a huge faux pas in their culture. You have to be very careful what you say and when you say it. When you are in a new country or even just a new environment, humor rarely translates.

Another time I was invited to the home of the Swiss experimental chef after we had traveled the markets together for months. Everybody in the office was oohing and aahing about the fact that he had invited me to his house and was going to cook a meal for me.

The main course was white asparagus with a beurre blanc sauce that he'd made from scratch. I didn't realize that this was one of the finest delicacies in the world, and that the white asparagus season in Switzerland is only two weeks long. Plus, for many great chefs, the true measure of a chef is his sauce. So what he did was actually spectacular, but I was sitting there thinking, "What is this? Where's the main course of the meal?"

I was gracious about it, but I wasn't overwhelmingly ebullient. When I came back to the office the next day, everyone asked about the meal.

"I was really a little disappointed," I said. "It was white asparagus with this special sauce."

My office friends looked at me as if I were a complete idiot, because I was clueless about how exceptional this meal had really been. Apparently everyone else in the office knew something I didn't, and once again I stepped in the wrong hole. Both of these were tremendous learning experiences. When you are working in a new environment, you can't assume your way is always the right way. If you go to another country assuming the American way is the only way, you'll never be successful.

One of the best lessons I learned was from a man named Rudy Tchan, a Swiss German who was the second-highest-ranking executive in Nestlé's Asian zone. He told me, "Don't assume that because a person doesn't speak English, he or she is not bright." Some of the brightest people I've ever met I needed a translator to talk to.

The key to limiting mistakes is to be really sensitive to people and try to understand what they're saying. But when you don't understand, ask questions rather than forming opinions on your own. And don't make jokes!

BYRON: TURNING OBSTACLES INTO MOTIVATION

When I left that game, I looked in the mirror and said, "That will never happen to me again. I will never be that frightened on a basketball court again."

When I was with the Lakers, there were plenty of hecklers. There was Leon the Barber in Detroit who would sit behind the bench about five rows up. He knew every player on the team, and he would call your name out and just talk. He knew stuff. Personal stuff.

Then there was a guy in DC, a lawyer who sat right behind the bench and just never let up. That guy heckled Charles Barkley one time and Chuck turned around and threw water at him.

In my playing days with the Lakers, there were always two places James Worthy didn't want to go, DC and Detroit. During shoot-around in DC, James would look around, and I could tell he was distracted by the thought of the heckling lawyer.

"He ain't coming tonight," I said. "It'll be cool."

"Aw, man, he probably is coming."

At the two-minute mark before the game started we were doing layups, and as soon as the buzzer rang, we turned around, looked over, and the guy was just taking his seat.

"James Worthy!" he yelled. "James Worthy! James Worthy, who do you have in your little black book here in Washington, DC?"

He heckled James the whole game. James finally turned around and just said to him, "Hey, man, I don't come to McDonald's and mess with you."

The guy just smiled at him and kept going for the rest of the night.

All of that is nothing compared to what I experienced in Greece, but after growing up in Inglewood, California, I knew I could handle anything. By the time we were back playing Peja's team again, I was talking and having a good time, mainly to show the crowd that they couldn't scare me. Every now and then I was giving them the finger right back.

I was back playing my game, but I'd be lying if I said it didn't mess me up at first. Outside forces can mess with your head. If you're supposed to be focused on winning, there will be people who try to stand in your way. When you're in a new environment, the opposition will do its best to make you uncomfortable.

But you can't intimidate me. That's not going to work. I'm sure there have been players who have packed their bags and just said, "Hell no," and walked out the door after game one. They don't want to deal with it, because it's scary. And they are right. The first time you go through something like that, it is scary. I will admit that.

Once you block out the noise (and the flying drachmas) it becomes just basketball again. Peja destroyed us in the first game, but when we met them again in the championship series, I guarded him. He still had a good night, but he didn't kill us as he had in the beginning. Even though I had a few years on him—I was almost twice his age at the time—I was still able to make him work for everything. He didn't beat me one-on-one off the dribble.

My energy and body language helped lift the other guys' play as well, and in the end we beat them 3–2 in the series and walked away champions. On a team where I'd started out feeling strange and out of place, by the end there was that familiar joy of success that made it all worthwhile.

CHARLIE: WINNING ON SOMEONE ELSE'S TURF

Many believe it's best to bring a person into your world when negotiating a business deal. Maybe there's an intimidation factor or some sort of power play that comes with sitting behind your big desk while the other person sits in a small chair on the other side. That was certainly the plan of the union heads when they invited me in to chat about a collective bargaining agreement with the water delivery drivers.

As a business leader, that's not how I operate. I find that I am more likely to get a deal done when I make the other person feel comfortable. I'll talk to them on their turf and walk away with what I want more often than not.

One time I was trying to buy a water company in the Central Valley in California. The owner of the business was reluctant; he felt we would not be good stewards of his employees because we were coat and tie, more sophisticated businessmen than he was accustomed to. His was a family business with maybe six or seven routes, so it had thirteen or fourteen employees in total.

He took us around to see the plant and the small headquarters, and introduced us to a number of people, but I wanted him to understand that we were no different from him. When it was time to make a deal, I said, "Let's just go sit on the back of your flatbed instead of being in a cramped office, and we'll talk about what you need for the business."

Dennis Blue, my head of route operations, was with me, and he was shocked when I said that. It was a tactic he had never seen before. Needless to say, we ended up sitting on the back of the flatbed and negotiating the deal.

I wanted it to be on his turf and on his terms. It's more comfortable for a route sales rep to talk to me if I'm riding the route with him in his truck than if he comes to my office. People are more insecure when they're outside their usual area.

By the time I got to Deer Park, I recognized that if I was going to be successful with what was largely a blue-collar workforce, I couldn't be the coat-and-tie person sitting behind a desk. I had to be able to get the employees to appreciate that I liked sports, that I wasn't afraid of doing manual labor, and that I could understand their problems. My efforts clearly resonated with people, and once that started, it snowballed.

Most of the water industry was made up of small companies, ones where the owner or the owner's parents had started the business, and they rode the route trucks. They were in the bottling plant. They were in the warehouse riding the forklift. They knew everything about that business from the ground up. I wanted them to understand that I also knew the business, and that they were talking to somebody who understood their concerns.

When you are a stranger in a strange land, you have to do your best to understand different cultures. If you're on the other side of the table and have the ability to make someone feel comfortable, you'll end up winning more times than not when you can adapt to their needs. Let the other person feel comfortable, and you're one step closer to making the deal on your terms.

X's and O's

- The rules may change in a new environment, but your confidence and work ethic must remain the same.

- Respecting other cultures is the first step to adapting to new surroundings.

- Turn obstacles into motivation instead of letting them knock you down.

- Making those around you feel comfortable facilitates a good outcome in almost any situation.

Chapter 10

Have a Mentor, Be a Mentor

"A mentor is someone who allows you to see the hope inside yourself." —Oprah Winfrey

Finding a person with more experience whom you trust and who can offer advice without judgment is a key component to making wise decisions in your career. A mentor will help you on many levels, and when it's your turn to become a mentor, trust that your help will go a long way.

BYRON: FOLLOWING THE ADVICE OF A MENTOR

After my time in Greece ended, I wasn't quite sure what my future held. One day while on the golf course with my former wife, I came to the realization that one thing I wasn't going to do was play basketball.

"I'm going to retire," I said before sending a tee shot straight down the fairway.

"What are you talking about?" she said. "You just won a championship over there."

"No, I'm done."

I knew I couldn't work out and get ready for the season in the way I normally do. I knew my body wasn't going to be able to handle it anymore. I tried, though. I tried working out, and my body said no. I had played fifteen years of professional basketball, and I just felt that this was the right time. I didn't want to be a guy who was hanging on just to be hanging on. I also didn't want to push myself to the point that it would affect my health later on in life. I'm able to run and work out and live life now because I walked away when I did.

"Well, do you think this is something we should talk about?"

"We don't need to talk about it," I said. "I'm retiring. It's over."

"What are we gonna do?"

During transition periods is when your relationships can really be tested the most. Throughout my playing career both Pat Riley and Larry Brown thought I would make a good coach. They both said it to me at various times.

My relationship with Larry dates back to high school. When I was thinking about playing college basketball I was choosing among UCLA, UNLV, and Arizona State. My mom wanted me to go to ASU and my dad wanted me to go to UCLA. I loved both schools, but then Jim Harrick, who was assistant coach at UCLA at the time, came to Morningside High School. UCLA had just fired Gary Cunningham, so Harrick was doing the recruiting while the school found a new head coach.

"We'll have a coach in the next week or so," he said, pointing his finger in my face. "Just understand this: people who don't go to UCLA don't beat UCLA."

Just like that, it was an easy decision. I was going to ASU.

A couple of days later they hired Larry Brown, who gave me a call and told me he really wanted me at UCLA. I wanted to play for him, but I had already committed to ASU and I wasn't going to go back on my word.

More than a decade later, when he was coaching the Pacers and I was a free agent in the NBA, I signed with the team. "I've been chasing you for years and I finally got you," he joked over dinner when we made it official. "I just need two things from you."

"What's that?"

"Your scoring off the bench and your leadership. Can you do that?"

From the beginning he was using me like a player/coach. During practices Coach Brown would ask, "How would you guys play the pick-and-roll back in the day?"

He knew the answers, of course, but he liked hearing what I had to say. "Well, Coach, we'd trap and push everything down to the baseline, or if it went in the post we would double-team…" And I'd lay out the scenarios.

"All right, let's do it that way," he said. "Let's try it."

It started my wheels turning about coaching, and that thought stayed in the back of my mind until that day on the golf course with my ex-wife.

"So what are we going to do?" she asked.

"I want to get into coaching," I said. "I'll put feelers out there, and if it doesn't happen this year, we're OK. We'll see about next year."

She got on board, and the next chapter began, but it was a chapter Larry Brown had already been writing for years.

CHARLIE: GUIDING A LEADER

There is a big difference between the roles of chairman of the board and CEO. Being chairman of the board is more like coaching, because you're working with fewer people and guiding their decision making. The board of directors is looking after the interests of the shareholders, whether it's a public company or a private company, and making sure that the management team is using the capital in an intelligent way, building plans for growth that are financeable, and hitting financial targets. You're not directly influencing the outcome; you're indirectly influencing the outcome.

A good board and a good chairman of that board engender a relationship with senior management so senior management feels that they can go to the board when they need something. In a sense the board plays a mentorship role—with the difference that it can replace a CEO if he or she is not doing a good job.

Scott Morris, one of the founders of Freshpet, was in his late thirties when he started the company. In 1989 he set the record at the Maccabiah Games in the 110-meter high hurdles, and I affectionately gave him the title of world's fastest Jew. At the University of North Carolina he ran track and was the ACC high jump champion. But above all that, he's terrifically knowledgeable in the pet food industry.

The issue Scott suffered from—like me early on—was that if people didn't get it right the first time, he'd just do the job himself. As Scott moved up in the organization, we talked many times about hiring people who could get the job done so that he didn't have to be the doer. Learning to hire capable people and trust those under him to get the job done helped Scott grow as a manager and leader in the organization. He was already one of the two or three most important people in the company, but now he's the president.

Issues continue to come up, and Scott's comfortable coming to me as the chairman of the board for advice. I welcome it. It's in my nature to want to help people in his position figure things out, and I think the company benefits from that.

When Scott was having issues of style and some substance with the CEO, I got involved to help them find a common ground. It's never about one person being right or wrong. It's always about something that both are doing that they need to be aware of, and it takes a third party—a mentor both people trust—to help them realize it's a two-way street.

At the end of the day, a board should not dictate. You can't take away from the CEO's or the president's responsibility to run the company, and, eventually, the best relationship is one in which the CEO or president understands that the board has to look out for the shareholders' best interests. While sometimes that might be in conflict with what management is trying to do, the board is ultimately there to help. But you're constantly negotiating and finding a middle ground where people believe that you're adding value.

The credibility that came with running successful businesses allowed me to be a person a CEO trusted. Plus I had some knowledge in consumer packaged goods from dealing with supermarkets and other retail outlets while working at Scott Paper, Nestlé, Clorox, and all the others through to McKesson. Over time, I think the management team found me to be a real ally and someone who was a partner in the business. They felt comfortable telling me the good, the bad, and the ugly. I trusted that they were good at what they did because they had been successful with Meow Mix before, and I protected them from shareholders or other partners when necessary. I knew that they were headed in the right direction, so the relationship worked.

BYRON: RELATIONSHIPS AND NEW OPPORTUNITY

Starting in my years in Indiana, I kept a journal of things I wanted to do offensively and defensively as a coach. I'd write down game situations and just sort of formulate plans for my future job. I took a lot of steps early on to prepare myself for the next phase of my career. I was a student of the game. But when it came to actually getting that opportunity, again it was a mentor who came through for me.

Amid my strenuous golf schedule, Jerry West and I started meeting once a week, having lunch together and talking about the Lakers' situation. They were looking for a new coach at that time.

"Whoever I hire, I'm going to see about you being on the staff," he said.

"That would be great," I said.

But they hired Phil Jackson and he had his own staff, so Jerry had a new plan.

"Young man," he said. He always called me *young man* no matter how old I got. "What I want you to do is come up to the front office and work with me."

"Jerry, thank you, that sounds great, but I'm not a suit guy right now," I said. "I want to be on the floor. I need to be on the floor."

Three or four days later I got a call from Geoff Petrie, the GM of the Sacramento Kings.

"We just hired Rick Adelman," he said. "Rick heard that you're looking to be a coach."

"Yes, how did you know?"

"Jerry West called us the other day," he said. "He told us if we don't hire you, he's going to find something for you."

I flew up to Sacramento and met with Rick and Geoff for about two hours, talking basketball. Rick was laid back and mellow and asked why I wanted to get into coaching and what I wanted my responsibilities to be.

"Whatever you want me to do, I'll do," I said. "I think I can really help young guys out. With my experience playing in this league for so many years, I feel I can really help the young guys."

They asked me about free agents. They were between Vlade Divac and Ike Austin. I told them I'd take Vlade.

"If you're putting him in with Webber, which is what I keep hearing," I said. "He's a great passer and unselfish. He's all about winning. He can score for you on the low post or bring guys out twenty feet. He can hit that shot."

They were concerned about his effort level, but with a veteran like him, if he takes eight games off a season, that's still seventy-four games that you'll get the good Vlade. To me that's worth it.

We finished the meeting and I was walking out when Adelman stopped me. "I tell you what," he said. "Why don't you take the weekend and think about it, but if you want the job, it's yours."

I flew home and told my ex-wife and she asked what I was going to do. "I'm going to call them tomorrow morning and tell them I want the job. They told me I can take the weekend, but I don't need the weekend."

CHARLIE: THE GRAY-HAIRED EXPERTS

Everyone needs a mentor who has some gray hair and who has been through it, because it's very hard if something you do blows up in your face. You need someone to tell you that you're not bad at your job and that you're going to learn from the blowup. Someone else who says, "Everybody makes mistakes," and who can talk to you in a nonjudgmental way and remind you that there are benefits to failure, is important to your success and growth as a businessperson. There is an enormous benefit in being able to share these experiences with someone who helps you look at the bigger picture and realize the advantages of a negative experience.

I had a number of wonderful bosses who really helped me—people such as Bernard Lebel, a Frenchman in Switzerland who was the head of the new products group at Nestlé headquarters. He was a great one to just sit and talk to about what was going on, what I was doing, and what I was learning. He had a lot of experience. He'd worked at Proctor & Gamble and had several very interesting jobs with different types of companies, and he could relate to what I was going through.

Bob Bolingbroke, the president of Clorox, was nonjudgmental and could look back on all his experiences and see what I was doing—the good and the bad—and help me sort through it. It was a huge decision to leave Clorox and head to McKesson, so I talked to Bob about the offer before I made the life change. I didn't want to leave him in the lurch, but I felt that the McKesson offer was a very compelling one. To run McKesson Water Products and be a corporate officer there seemed like a great opportunity, and Bob said that I should take that position.

He thought I had the potential to really rise within Clorox and that I was one of a handful of people he thought could eventually be a candidate for president of the company. But he couldn't offer me anything at the time that would compare to the opportunity at McKesson, and so he knew it would be in my best interests to take it.

Having a boss like that is invaluable. Being a boss like that is admirable. When you are running a successful company, you should be able to look outside the box and be supportive of the people working for you. Being a good mentor means looking beyond what's best for you and focusing on what's best for the person you are working with.

Bob is an honest person, and he was successful because of it. I trusted his opinion because he had been nothing but honest with me from the day we met. If he said take the job—or, more importantly, if he said don't take the job—I knew his answer was coming from the right place.

People who put their own ego first and get angry when an employee says, "I have this other opportunity" are not doing anyone any favors. Bob wasn't like that, and he was a better leader for it.

To this day I still call Bob when I have an issue and I need advice. He's a friend and a peer, but he'll always be a mentor. Our relationship has always remained the same because, even as a boss, he didn't treat me as his subordinate. He treated me as a partner, and we would discuss issues and brainstorm around them rather than his dictating the course to me.

It's hard for some people in Bob's position to be that kind of person. They work so hard to become the boss that they forget that a true leader should guide and help instead of demand and demean. But if you've spent your life having a mentor, you should remember what it takes to become a good mentor yourself. When you do, everyone wins.

BYRON: CREATING A MODEL FOR SUCCESS

While mentors help you move forward in your career, they also provide the foundation for how you'll do the job. By the time I started in Sacramento, my coaching journal was pretty thick— filled with stuff I'd learned from Pat Riley and Larry Brown about basketball schemes and on-court decisions. But I also learned how to treat players from them and guys like Jerry West as well.

I loved Pat Riley's determination and his work ethic, and the way he would just poke you to make sure he got the very best out of you. I loved the way Larry Brown treated you like family. He was like the father you didn't want to disappoint. Jerry West was a straight shooter. He told it like it was and you always respected him for his honesty.

Then, of course, working under Rick Adelman I watched and learned too. Rick was a laid-back player's coach who delegated authority. He had a CEO-on-the-court type of feel. Mix the Riley, Brown, and Adelman styles and characteristics together and that's the coach I knew I wanted to be.

You can be a mentor as a player, especially toward the end of your career, but when you are the coach you basically have to be the mentor, otherwise you're not doing your job.

In my two seasons with Sacramento (the first one shortened due to a lockout) we had some excellent teams. The team signed Vlade as I'd suggested in my interview, and also signed Peja Stojakovic, whom I'd played against in Greece. They drafted Jason "White Chocolate" Williams and traded for Chris Webber, who was not happy about joining the team at first.

He was a great player—great in the post, great passer, soft hands, great rebounder, and guys enjoyed playing with him—so we wanted him to be happy.

As a coach and leader, you start by showing the player a lot of love. Let him know that he's really wanted, tell him you believe in him, and make sure he knows that this team will go only as far as he can take it.

Rick did a great job of getting Webber's confidence high and saying to him right away, "You're the best player on this team, and you're going to have a great career here."

This was a fresh start for Webber, a fresh start for us, and we were all just trying to be as positive as possible with him, just to show him that this could be a pretty good situation for him.

As soon as we started winning, he saw that playing with Vlade was great because Vlade had the same type of unselfish mentality that he had, and that Jason Williams was also a pass-first type of guy. Peja could just shoot the lights out. When things started to click, Webber started becoming a vocal leader, took his own game to the next level, and enjoyed his best seasons as a professional with the Kings.

In my first season with the team we lost to the Jazz in the playoffs, and the following year we met, of course, Kobe Bryant, Shaquille O'Neal, and the Los Angeles Lakers, who took us out in a tough battle in the first round on the way to winning the 2000 NBA championship.

I don't think Jerry West even cared that he was getting me a job at what would become a big interstate rival in those years. I looked at him as my "basketball dad," and I think he was just looking out for his basketball son. He knew I wanted to coach, and so he was going to help make that happen. That's all that mattered to him.

Webber and the team went on to develop a great rivalry with the Lakers over the next few years. After that second season, I was ready to become a head coach.

CHARLIE: CULTURAL CONNECTIONS

When I'm hiring I'm looking for someone who obviously has the right skill set and has shown success in prior work environments. I'm really interested in seeing not only success over an extended period, but also leadership skills in whatever roles they've had. That's critical.

You really want somebody you feel is honest and isn't selling, but rather explaining what they've been doing. I'm also interested in getting references from people they have worked for, people they have worked with, and people that they have managed. You learn a whole lot when you get down a couple of levels.

I also like to see people who acknowledge having made mistakes and talk about what they've learned from them. It's really important to know what they did well and what they didn't do well. When people say they've never made a mistake, to me that's a huge red flag, because anybody who's taking risks makes mistakes. You want to own those mistakes as much as you want to own the success you've had.

All these characteristics are important for adding the right person to your working environment, and they set the tone for a good mentoring or CEO-manager relationship.

I need to be confident that the person will fit in with the culture of the company, and the employee should feel the same way.

When Clorox bought Deer Park and we were folded into that company, I was concerned about the culture at first. It was a really buttoned-up kind of organization. Bob Bolingbroke was an elder in the Mormon Church and had a reputation as a serious-minded guy, so even before I met Bob, there was this image of him as being someone you couldn't have fun around.

In the water industry, a few things were very popular. One was liar's poker. Another was going to the bar and drinking mudslides. When my partners and I were negotiating to sell Deer Park to Clorox with our attorney in this big conference room at Clorox's headquarters in Oakland, I didn't know what to expect, because the water industry was one way and the Clorox team seemed to be the complete opposite.

My partners—Jim Land, third-generation owner of the Wissahickon Spring Water Company outside Philadelphia, and Bill Bell, who had his own water company, Tyler Mountain of Pittsburgh— were both salt-of-the-earth guys. Bill started out in the warehouse as a forklift operator. Jim had been a route driver. They were water industry guys through and through.

Bill had brought a briefcase full of one-dollar bills to play liar's poker, and while we were waiting for Bob we were playing in the conference room at Clorox's headquarters. Bob walked in and we just continued to play our game. He instantly had a big smile on his face, and he asked, "What is that?"

Within four months of our closing the deal, he was closing his office door and playing conference call liar's poker with us from across the country. Bill would be in Pittsburgh, Jim in Philadelphia, I in New York, and Bob in Oakland, and we played liar's poker on the phone. Why everyone else had been so nervous about him, I have no clue, but we hit it off right from the very beginning. With him there was no BS. He did what he said he would do, he listened and gave sound advice, and he was not a judgmental person.

He was a guy I wanted to work with, and even if he didn't go the extra mile and become a mentor, he possessed all the leadership qualities to inspire a guy like me to become a leader. Whether you are hiring or you are the one looking to join a company, those qualities go hand in hand. You should hire someone who fits the mold of a leader, and you should want to work in a place where leadership is encouraged. If a mentoring relationship develops, that's a bonus.

X's and O's

- When making a leap to a new position, find guidance from those whom you trust and who believe in your ability to succeed.

- Use your knowledge to guide people to success instead of taking on the task yourself.

- Be the boss you wish you had.

- Someone who fits in with the culture and feels encouraged to lead will be your biggest asset.

Chapter 11

Building from the Bottom Up

"Where you start should not determine where you end up." —Barack Obama

When you have to start from scratch and build a winner from the bottom up, it's best to do it with honesty and integrity. To create a winning culture, it helps to remember that every person on the team plays an important role in that success.

BYRON: SEARCHING FOR LEADERS

After my second season as an assistant coach with the Kings ended, I got four calls about head coaching jobs—in Indiana, Vancouver, Atlanta, and New Jersey. When you're an assistant on a team on the rise, you quickly become the "next big thing" in coaching. To them I was that guy who'd thought like a coach when he was a player and now thought like a player as a coach. That's exciting for a team looking to make a change. It was an opportunity I wanted to seize, but it was hard for me to go on the job interviews because I'm a very loyal person. Rick Adelman was supportive, though, and I ended up taking the job with the New Jersey Nets.

I wanted to go to a team that I could build into a champion franchise, and I liked the players that they had in New Jersey, but mainly I liked the team's flexibility. It wasn't tied to any bad contracts, and all the players could be moved if necessary.

In my two years with the Kings I really studied Rick and everything he did, and compared his performance to how some of my previous coaches had handled the role of head coach. I saw how he went through his pregame speech, how he went through halftime routines, and how he handled postgame. I watched the way he handled matchups and drew up plays, and how he broke down video to the team. I tried to study everything and felt that would help me in the long run. Once I was in the head job, it felt natural to me. Everything felt right. I did have to buy nicer suits, though.

Once I joined the team, my goal was to win games, but also to really plan for the future. I knew from day one this first-season roster wasn't going to be a championship-caliber team, so I wanted to spend time and see who was a winner and who was not. We had some big names on the team that first year—guys like Stephon Marbury, Keith Van Horn, Stephen Jackson, Sherman Douglas, and a rookie by the name of Kenyon Martin.

I came in strong, probably a little too strong, but that's all I knew at that time. I come from the Pat Riley school of coaching, so I went in with an iron fist right away and had guys throwing up and damn near falling out at training camp just doing what in LA we'd called the easy run. Kendall Gill said it was the hardest first day he'd ever had in his life in the NBA, and he had been in the league for a decade at the time.

I wanted to come in and establish myself as a taskmaster, because that was the total opposite of what they had had there before. I went a little overboard on a couple of occasions. I came in with the right attitude, but the approach was too strong. What worked on me as a player doesn't necessarily work on everyone. I don't think I lost respect from any of the guys. I just think they looked at me as if I were crazy.

As a coach you get only one shot at making your first impression, and they were going to know me as hardworking and tough minded. The practices weren't going to be easy, but the guys were going to be prepared. That's what I wanted them to know. I needed them to understand what a championship-level work ethic looked like, because the ones who were around the following year needed to have a year of that experience under their belts.

We finished that first season 26–56, well out of playoff range. Late in the season Gill came into my office. He and I had played against each other a bit, and we had a mutual respect.

"Coach," he said, "if I can make a suggestion, get rid of everybody."

In my mind I had already erased guys that I felt didn't need to be there the next year, but when a player came in and said that, it just made me laugh.

"Tell me what you really think," I joked.

"You have to just start over."

"I hear you."

"If not," he said, "you're not going to win."

He was right.

CHARLIE: GIVING EVERYONE A VOICE

If you step into a new situation and rule with an iron fist, you're going to get a lot of pushback. Byron was trying to get the most out of his players and see which ones had the will to win. He tested them physically, but he didn't have a my-way-or-the-highway approach. That's why Kendall Gill was comfortable enough to come to him. He respected Byron.

When I got to McKesson I was in the same position. I knew I'd be starting from scratch and I had to weed out the unnecessary people on my roster. So what I did was have the management team start task forces that took people from various departments within the company and had them come back with recommendations on how to consolidate.

They had a platform for talking to us directly about what they thought was going well and what they thought wasn't going well. For the first time senior management was actually listening to them and concerned about what they had to say.

I believe that there are very few people who really are looking to take advantage of you. Most people are honest, they want to work hard, and they're going to tell you what's smart, what's going well, and what's going poorly, if they feel you care. If you get under the surface with people, you'd be amazed at the richness of what's there. In the best-performing companies, on the best-performing sports teams, everybody believes that they're in this together and they aren't being taken advantage of. They're part of a family and part of a team. If you can create that culture, you're going to be so far ahead of the competition.

Later on we created focus groups of employees from all over the company to make suggestions about what was and wasn't working within the corporation. We took our best and brightest and put them in these focus groups to make decisions about the future of the company.

It was an honor for people to be invited to the focus groups. They were really charged up when I would come in with several of the senior managers.

Success starts with active listening and with understanding the things that are going well with the employees and the customers. So we'd ask what suggestions they had regarding what we weren't doing, and what we could be doing better for the customer. Asking midlevel and frontline employees what will be helpful to the company is really the best way to fix a company, because they see things in a way that upper management will never understand on their own.

When we were closer to restructuring the company and, ultimately, laying off a thousand people, I went to Arizona to meet with the senior team there because I knew they were honest, hardworking guys who had worked in a number of different places for the company.

I sat in the backyard of the head of the strategic business unit—a man who had been with the company ever since he moved to the United States from the former Yugoslavia. Along with him were the head of manufacturing and the head of route operations for that region. I told them what I was thinking strategy-wise, about combining the strategic business units and eliminating a number of jobs. They were all hardworking, no-nonsense guys, and they all looked at me and said that I had to do it.

"We don't know whether we're going to have a job, but we've got to be honest about it," they said. Just as Kendall Gill did with Byron, they put the team first. I knew I could trust them, and they were all given opportunities to continue to grow within the company. The head of route operations for one particular division ended up running the route operations for the whole company.

A lot of strategy goes into getting the most out of people. Asking for their honest opinions is usually a good start.

BYRON: REBUILDING THE ROSTER

Of course, we couldn't get rid of everyone before the next season. There were plenty of solid guys on the team. Kenyon had just finished his rookie year and had come from a winning tradition at the University of Cincinnati, Aaron Williams had a winning attitude and was a real company guy, and Lucious Harris was a very talented basketball player who we knew could perform well with the right guys around him. Keith Van Horn was just talented as hell. He was a stretch four before everyone was talking about stretch fours, and Kenyon was a physical presence who could do things in the paint. Together they were a force to be reckoned with.

Stephon Marbury was a very good scoring point guard, but the guys didn't like playing with him. He was a shoot-first guard with a me-first attitude. That didn't go over well in the locker room. Kerry Kittles was hurt that first season, but years later I was told the truth, and that was that he didn't want to play with Marbury. Had I known that was the case I wouldn't have been happy about it, and would have either pushed him to play or gotten rid of him altogether, but his trick knee kept acting up, so he sat out the season.

With the guys we had in place that second season, we felt we needed an old-school point guard who was a pass-first guy to lead this team. Somebody who would get the other guys the ball, somebody the guys would trust and respect.

When Rod Thorn came to me and asked if I would trade Stephon for Jason Kidd, I said, "Yeah, I'll take the trade, and if you want me to, I'll drive him there and drive Jason back here." A week later the trade was made. We felt great in our organization. We had a serious piece of the puzzle. Kidd was one of the best point guards in the league at the time, and everyone knew it. He brought a lot of the intangibles we needed.

Kidd wasn't a very vocal leader, but he led by example. He practiced hard and played hard, and guys just followed his lead. When he came to us from Phoenix, he had been an all-star a couple of times, so the guys had respect from day one.

At our first meeting at the team dinner, I pulled him to the side before we even went in, before training camp started, and I said, "Listen, when we go in here tonight, I'm going to speak to the team, and I'm going to introduce you as the team captain. So I just want to prepare you if you want to say a few words. If you don't, that's fine, but I want everybody to know that you are the leader."

He spoke about the season, what he was expecting, and how happy he was to be there. The guys were just glued to him when he spoke. It was a quick speech that wrapped with, "Let's get to work tomorrow," but it energized the guys. Kerry Kittles's knee was feeling much better all of a sudden. Once we had Kidd, Kittles and everyone in the organization knew that this team could be something special.

CHARLIE: BUILDING ENTHUSIASM IN A NEW TEAM

I knew that we had to centralize all the individual strategic business units—mini companies run in each territory—from the second I got there, but once I had the consulting firm and the focus groups and guys like my team in Arizona tell me, then we were ready to make the move.

Even after I had gone to them to ask them what was working and what wasn't working, I felt I needed to have some influencers supporting what I wanted to get accomplished. After we made the changes, I didn't want morale to sink among the remaining employees. The ones left needed to know the change was a good thing, so I had to go about this in the right way.

I went and spoke to individual people from different regions of the country who I thought were well respected in their areas, and tried to explain my strategy. I had three different constituencies I needed to win over—the route sales reps who were delivering the product to the end user, the plant workers who were making the product, and the customer service reps who were dealing with customers. Then I also had to convince middle and senior management that I deserved to be in that role when several of them thought they should have my job.

Like a politician going door-to-door, I went out and started talking about what was working and what was not working, and why the current system was not cost effective. I had spent months listening to everyone, and now it was time for them to listen to me.

I got a number of the key influencers in the organization behind me before we went forward with the organizational change. They could then talk about the benefits of the changes so others weren't hearing about them just from me or other senior management at corporate. Since you need a motivated workforce, you have to have the team eventually understand what you're trying to accomplish and how you're trying to accomplish it, and it works better when they aren't always hearing it from one person. Having the right people on your side makes the transition significantly easier.

To let everyone know I was serious about the success of the company and caring for it on every level, I made a point of riding along on routes and delivering half the bottles myself. If we had an objective of getting two new accounts in a day, I would be knocking on doors and having a fun competition with the route sales rep to see who could get more new accounts that day. I would do one side of the street and he or she would do the other side. I'd do it in Arizona in the summertime and have them turn the air conditioning off in the trucks because I liked to sweat.

I went to the plants and I worked on the lines with the people. I would get there right when they opened. They'd look at me and have no idea what I was doing there.

"I want to learn what you're doing, and I want to be able to do it with you," I'd say.

I went to the call centers and I took calls from customers. We had an escalating system on calls, so if a customer service rep couldn't satisfy the customer who was calling, he or she could escalate it to their supervisor. If the supervisor couldn't resolve the issue, it could go all the way up to me. Any call that came to me I saw as an opportunity to win over a customer, not just to answer the immediate question. I'd find out what the caller really thought about our organization and then show them why they were making the right decision being with us.

After I'd been doing all of this for a while, people said, "You know, this guy is doing what he's preaching, across the board." They liked my energy and the newfound energy within the company. Even though a thousand people were let go, most of the remaining 1,500 were excited about their jobs and the future of McKesson Water. Instead of the reorganization feeling like a setback, morale stayed positive and everyone was working to the best of their ability.

There was certainly some survivor guilt among the remaining employees, so we had to work hard to overcome that. I think everyone realized that had we not eliminated the thousand positions, everyone would have eventually lost their job, and the company would not have survived in its independent state. Knowing this, people worked hard with a positive attitude, and when we rebuilt back to a staff of 2,500, everyone felt that they were part of something special.

BYRON: WINNING ADJUSTMENTS

Charlie's got 2,500 employees to deal with. As a coach, I have 15 guys, but he and I have the same goals when trying to motivate. When each player is playing to best of his ability and the chemistry is there among the guys, we can win and win big. I have to get to know them and they have to get to know me for it all to work. At the end of the day, I want them to look at me and know I'm here to help them get better as basketball players and enhance their careers.

We got off to a great start that season. Everyone started believing and buying into the system. All of a sudden those hard practices didn't seem so hard anymore. Winning cures everything. It changes the whole environment.

The guys loved each other, played for each other, and trusted each other. They also trusted me, which was very important. That confidence led us to a 52–30 record, good for the number one seed in the Eastern Conference. It was one of the greatest turnarounds in NBA history.

In the playoffs we battled against Indiana and Charlotte to face the Boston Celtics in the Eastern Conference Finals. They owned us in the regular season and were up 2–1 on us in the series when I decided to make an adjustment. We'd originally had Kenyon Martin guarding Paul Pierce, but, for whatever reason, he just couldn't figure out how to guard him. K-Mart was our best defender, so I knew it frustrated him.

So I made a switch and put Kerry Kittles on Pierce and moved

Kenyon to Antoine Walker. It worked out well in both regards, because it slowed down Pierce and shut down Walker. Kittles was longer and probably a little bit quicker laterally, so he gave Pierce problems. Kenyon was strong, so Walker couldn't get inside, and nearly every time Antoine took the ball up to shoot, Kenyon would get his hand on it. That switch allowed us to dominate the rest of the series, but it wouldn't have happened if we weren't a perfectly unified team with a winning attitude.

Kenyon didn't complain about the switch or play with his head down. He looked at covering Antoine Walker as a challenge. Kittles was happy to take on Pierce, and both guys went and played their hearts out. That effort and that attitude started that first practice of the first season I was there. They might have been puking, but the practice made them strong both physically and mentally, and brought out the winner within them.

We beat the Celtics that year and went to the NBA Finals, where the lights were just a little too bright for the guys. They usually are for a team that gets there for the first time—especially a team that didn't even make the playoffs the year before. There was joy in getting there because we had come so far.

I'll give you one guess as to whom we lost to in the Finals. That's right, the Los Angeles Lakers. It's hard enough to win a championship, but to do it against a franchise with winning ingrained in its culture is damn near impossible.

CHARLIE: UPSIDE-DOWN ORGANIZATION

My whole plan of restructuring was based on what is called upside-down organization. Most organizations have the CEO at the top, above the other different layers in the company, down to the frontline people at the bottom—like a pyramid. I like to flip that model on its head and have the frontline people at the top and the CEO at the bottom.

I would always say the most important people in the organization for us are the frontline people, because they are the ones dealing every day with the customers. Whether they're route sales reps or customer service reps, they're hearing every day what the customers are saying—the good and the bad. That's why I spent so much time with the frontline people. They needed to know that I didn't just value them, I considered them the most important people in the company.

When I started to get the whole organization to think in that way, it unlocked all kinds of great learning opportunities for us. We went from being a command-and-control company, before I got there, to being an organization where everybody had an opportunity to improve the company.

As for me, I viewed my role as that of facilitator for the frontline people so they could do their jobs better. I got rid of the only reserved parking space in the parking lot, which was for the CEO, and the company's exclusive membership at the Jonathan Club. The company was a blue-collar organization, and I didn't want a divide between the executives and the front line. Again, they were the most important, and I wanted them to know I knew it.

My role was to make sure they had the training, the skills, and the tools to do their jobs, and to ensure that as a company we were not making their jobs harder. We took away the non-value-added work that was taking up part of the day so they could spend their entire day delivering water, opening new accounts, collecting open receivables, or doing whatever they had to do.

For example, when I got there a typical route supervisor received

1,200 pages of reports a month. Nobody is going to read 1,200 pages of reports a month. Nobody is going to get halfway through it. We ended up going from 1,200 pages to one page per route rep of key indicators. That's all a supervisor needed to manage any given route rep's day. So the managers and the reps were not bogged down with paperwork, and that freed up many hours to be more productive and make money for the company.

The route reps were on an incentive-based pay scale, so when we made life easier, productivity was at an all-time high. Once we changed the mind-set, the ripple effect could be seen throughout the organization.

When I got to McKesson Water Products, the customer service group was rated by how many phone calls it could take per hour. The people who took the most phone calls per hour were considered the best performers. We switched our strategy to trying to eliminate calls, not take more. We started to measure how many of the customers had to call a second time. We had the data to track that. Customer service is about issue resolution, not about how many calls you can take in a day. It made the company far better in the eyes of both the end user and our team. Before, team members had hurried to end a call quickly so they could take another call. Now they were spending a few extra minutes and trying to solve problems.

Whether it's on the basketball court or in the workplace, people want to be challenged, but they want to know that a victory means something. That's why I was always putting them first. When employees wanted company assistance with further education, or more exposure to other areas of the operation so they could someday advance, I tried my best to make it happen.

We also pushed the importance of helping the community. Every one of the operating units was given a certain amount of money annually that it could use to make charitable contributions. That was important to people. When we had tragedies such as the Northridge earthquake, our people were proud that the company was giving back to the community. See, when you create an upside-down organization and put the frontline worker at the top, that worker takes it to the next level and makes the customer and the community the top priorities. That's the way the company can truly be successful.

X's and O's

- When new to a leadership role, you have to earn respect all over again.

- Giving a voice to those below you is a key component to getting the most out of them.

- Build support before you make a move that will change the direction of the team.

- Flip your organizational pyramid upside down and treat the frontline people as the most important.

Chapter 12

Delegating Authority and Providing Options

"No man will make a great leader who wants to do it all himself, or to get all the credit for doing it." —Andrew Carnegie

When running an organization, you'll never be able to do every job by yourself. You need to find a team you trust and mold them into producers who in the best-case scenario will eventually follow in your footsteps.

BYRON: MATCHING TEACHER WITH TALENT

When I got the head coaching job in New Jersey, I was building a staff for the first time. Being the boss is a big transition from playing and being an assistant coach. Now I was doing the hiring and firing and delegating authority. In the past I'd had a job and I'd done that job to the best of my ability. Now I had to do a job and not only make sure others were doing theirs, but also help define their roles.

I got lucky because Eddie Jordan was already there when I got to

New Jersey. Eddie and I had known each other for years. As a matter of fact, when I got traded from the Clippers to the Lakers, it was for Eddie Jordan and Norm Nixon.

When I got to the Nets and interviewed him for the assistant coaching job, I felt very comfortable with him. I was confident that he would be an asset to us. He knew some of the players and he knew a little bit of what was going on in the organization. I knew that would be very helpful to me. Michael O'Koren was a good friend of Eddie's who was there as well, and I really loved his personality, his work ethic, and the way he handled the big guys. Then I brought in Lawrence Frank, who was recommended to me by both Stu Jackson and Kurt Rambis. I interviewed him just before he went on his honeymoon, and called him mid–romantic getaway to tell him he'd gotten the job.

I had no problem bringing guys in at work and talking to them and telling them what their responsibilities were going to be if I hired them. The role of the assistant has changed over the years, but for the most part assistant coaches serve as the middlemen and -women between the players and the head coach. When I was an assistant I wasn't far removed from my playing days, so the guys saw me as one of them. It's amazing how quickly that changes when you become the head coach.

No matter how long it's been since an assistant coach was playing, a special connection between player and assistant coach is necessary for success. Paul Pressey, for example, who was an assistant coach with me in a number of places, is more than twenty years removed from his playing days, but he still has a way about him that makes players feel comfortable. I wouldn't have him on the floor working out players, because that's not his thing anymore, but he's an expert at making sure that everybody is on the same page. He's also great at putting out the little fires and quieting the cackling before it gets to me and talking players off the ledge. To a head coach that asset is invaluable.

As a head coach the first thing you learn is that you can't handle everything. If an assistant coach can come in and carry some of that load, then I can think about the big picture and map out the road to a championship.

The one thing I did a bit differently from most was that I didn't divide players by position. Instead I let them gravitate to the coaches they felt a connection to and let the relationships develop naturally. For instance, when I was an assistant coach in Sacramento I was in charge of the guards, since I was a former guard. So I was in charge of Vernon Maxwell, Jason Williams, Peja Stojakovic, Nick Anderson, and the others. In practice we worked on ball handling, footwork, shooting setups, and things of that nature, since those were my specialty.

Rick Adelman didn't tell me what to do, he just said, "You got the guards." It was better for me as a coach, because every day I had to formulate a workout plan for all those guys and make sure everyone was on the same page.

When I became a head coach I decided that instead of putting the point guards together with a coach who was a former point guard, I'd have everyone out on the floor at the beginning of the season and just watch to see whom the players gravitated toward. A lot of times it worked out the same, but every now and then some of the guards gravitated toward a guy who was more of a forward or center coach, and vice versa. To me, if you're a coach, you're a coach. You can coach bigs, you can coach guards—it doesn't matter. It's basketball, and it's more important for players to be around someone they feel comfortable working with than it is to lump everyone into a group before getting to know them. It's part of delegating authority, and for me it has always worked.

CHARLIE: TRANSITIONING FROM DOER TO SUPERVISOR

Delegating authority is probably one of the toughest tasks a rising leader in the business world has to learn to do. Throughout your life you're a doer. You're given a job or you create an opportunity for yourself, and you go and make it happen.

From a young age, I always had goals. As soon as it started to snow, I was already thinking about shoveling eight driveways per day. Depending on the size of the driveway, I might get two or three dollars to do it, and I didn't care if I had to stay out until eight o'clock at night, I was going to stay out until I got twenty dollars. That was my mind-set as a kid, and it carried me all the way until my days at Nestlé, when I realized I had to make a change.

My first project in the United States with Nestlé was a product called Choco-Chill, a cocoa powder that was like Nesquik, except that instead of adding milk you added water. It was a summertime alternative to fruit-based drinks.

The head of the department wanted to go national with it, but I did some early research and I was afraid that it was going to be a huge failure. First I got him to agree to test half the country, then a third of the country, and finally, when I got him to 12 percent, he put his foot down.

I had somebody reporting to me, one of these people who want to please everybody, and he was afraid to tell the head of the department that the research wasn't terribly positive. Instead of sending him back to do it, I dealt with it.

The same happened when I was involved in a project called New

Cookery, a precursor to Lean Cuisine. On a couple of occasions I was overly critical of the presentations my direct reports were doing, rather than being encouraging. I was looking for what was wrong with the presentation rather than what was right with it.

None of these people liked me very much as a supervisor, and rightly so. I was the one who was not doing his job correctly. At some point in life, if you want to be a leader, you have to make the transition from shoveling snow to motivating others to do the shoveling.

It wasn't an easy transition, and early on I wasn't a good manager because I was so much of a doer. If I asked somebody to do something and that person didn't get it done right, I would just take over and do it myself.

When the president of Nestlé USA asked me to run Deer Park, it was the first time I had a whole company beneath me. I had to worry about receivables and payables and cash flow, and it was impossible to do everything myself. On top of that, we had branches in multiple states and we had a real initiative to grow through acquisition. So it was far more complex than what I was used to.

I could do only so much by myself, and I realized that I wasn't going to get other people to do it the way I did it. I had to back off and find a way to motivate people to want to do the best they could. That was when the lightbulb went on in my head showing me that I was going to get the best out of people if they felt that I really cared about what they were doing.

It was a turning point in my career as a leader, and from that point on I dedicated myself to finding the right people for the job, molding them into leaders, and caring about their progress and success as if they were my own.

BYRON: CHAMPIONSHIP-LEVEL LEADERS ARE EVERYWHERE

When you're an organization on the path to a championship, the entire team plays a big role. It's not just the coaches or players but everyone on staff, from the president or GM down to the administrative assistants working for the team. That's why so many people get rings when we do win. When you're in it you realize how important every person is.

In a championship-level organization such as the Los Angeles Lakers there are guys like trainer Gary Vitti. He arrived in my second season and we clicked right away. I told him I needed to get stronger and he was like, "Cool, we'll start lifting weights." Back then lifting weights was sort of frowned upon, but I did it anyway because he promised me it would work. But then Jerry West stepped in.

"Jerry just had a meeting with me and told me that I'm going to ruin you," Vitti said. "He's old school. He doesn't believe in lifting weights, and he told me that I'm going to ruin you."

Then Vitti, the half-pint Tom Selleck Italian stallion, just looked at me and said, "So what do you want to do?"

I loved that about him. He was new with the team, a young guy with a big curly Afro and thick mustache, and it didn't matter that his boss was telling him to stop. He wanted to do whatever the player wanted to do.

"I want to lift," I said, and we kept on going. When we got to training camp that next season I had gained about ten pounds of muscle and everyone was impressed. It didn't affect my shooting or stamina or anything else. The next year, when we were in Hawaii, Gary and I went to World's Gym to work out with Magic and three others. All of a sudden most of the guys wanted to lift weights. Jerry still thought it was crazy, but it worked out for all of us. He didn't fire Gary. He let him do his thing and trusted him as a trainer to make the right training decisions.

A person who doesn't understand team chemistry may just say, "Hey, we can get any trainer. We don't need some guy who is going to go against our wishes in the training room." But Jerry knew better. Gary Vitti was so much more to that organization. For me he was a guy I could talk to about life—not only the issues that occurred on the court but whatever was happening in my personal life as well. If I was having a problem, I could go to Gary, and he always had great advice, even when he was a young guy. I was very moody when I played basketball, so if we lost a game I was pissed. He was always talking sense into me and telling me to not take the game home with me. He was there to help at every turn, and everyone who has put on the Lakers uniform in the past thirty years probably has a similar story.

A guy like Gary is essential for winning, and he made a number of guys both better basketball players and better men. In thirty years with the Lakers he was a vital part of the team, and part of what made him so valuable was that he was given the reins to be a leader. Management let Gary be Gary, and in his time he won eight championship rings.

CHARLIE: A PARTNER IN SUCCESS

The people you surround yourself with end up defining your success in business. Sometimes you have to go out and find the right people. At Deer Park I convinced a very competent young marketing executive and a smart financial person to come over from Nestlé. And of course my two partners, Jim Land and Bill Bell, each had a lifetime of experience in the water industry.

I'm always looking to surround myself with the best people in whatever I'm doing. One of the greatest qualities a leader can have is to know what they know and also know what they don't know. A good leader is able to say, "I need to find the best person I can for this, because I'm not really good at it."

At Deer Park I had a support group around me who had many years of experience and success—people who knew more than I knew, and I recognized that. That helped me become much more successful, and in the process started me on the path of seeing how the right leadership can truly motivate people.

Sometimes you get lucky and inherit the best in the business. At McKesson Water we had Linda Rush as our head of Human Resources. She was an expert at her job, and oftentimes she was pretty good at my job too. As I mentioned before, she was my psychiatrist during the restructuring of the company.

Quite a few people were not on board with the changes at McKesson Water. Some people created an underground newsletter poking fun at me and my work style. Others sent angry anonymous letters. It was brutal at times, and Linda was there through it all to calm my reaction to these letters, and to pour me a drink from time to time.

I tried numerous times to explain why we were doing what we were doing. If someone was not on board, it showed in their performance and dragged down the team, so they had to go. Linda was always on top of that and as a team player could spot the bad seeds almost immediately.

She was also the moderator of the focus groups that helped discover and fix a lot of the problems in the company. She would go in and talk to a select group and turn their concerns into positive questions for senior management to discuss with the group. We were ending the sessions by resolving issues rather than just taking the complaints and calling it a day. Sometimes we were able to fix the problem and sometimes we weren't, but the team always left happy because their voices had been heard and their frustrations were for the most part eliminated. Linda really made that happen with the way she cared for the employees and the way she conducted business in these focus groups and throughout the workday.

Part of the problem with many leaders is that they're working two levels below where they should be working. When you're in the weeds, everyone's working two or three levels below where they should be because they have to find a space where they can be productive. But if I move down and do your job, then you're going to move down and do a lower-level job too. You're never going to get out from under a poorly performing company, because nobody will be working at the appropriate level.

If you're doing that as a CEO, you become so caught up in the day-to-day of the business that you're not sitting back and thinking about how to make it a better business. You spend the whole day putting out fires and don't have time to step back and help the business grow. With Linda and other strong executives at my side, I was able to avoid that trap. Instead of focusing on the problems of today, I was able to do my job and concentrate on how the company could be better tomorrow.

BYRON: EMBRACE THE SUCCESSOR

A lot goes into putting together a winning team of coaches. When I hire an assistant coach, I need to know right away if he wants to be a head coach. Then I have to make a decision: Do I trust that he's not backstabbing me, trying to get my job?

In nine years working with Paul Pressey, I knew he didn't want to be a head coach. It was a lot easier for me knowing that he was content with his role, though at the same time I love for the younger assistants to get that chance if they want it. I want them to learn from me as much as possible, and then hopefully one day they'll get an opportunity and they'll seize the moment just as I did.

But once I was in Rick Adelman's position, it became hard to focus on the main goal when rumblings were going on about where the assistants might end up. When I was in New Jersey, Eddie Jordan had a few teams interested in talking to him. He was good about not letting it interfere with what we were trying to do. When the buzzing started he came to me and said he wouldn't focus on it until after the season, and he stayed true to his word. We were trying to win a championship and he cared more about the team than about his own future career. That's important for a player, and also a good quality for a future head coach to have. He ended up taking the job with the Washington Wizards, and I was happy for him because DC is a place where he has roots, and I thought he would do a good job.

We made two trips to the NBA Finals, and halfway through my fourth season as head coach with the Nets, management decided my time was up. The man who had brought us together, Jason Kidd, was one of the guys who ended up tearing us apart. He and a few other guys decided they wanted a change, and it's a player's league, so I was out the door.

That was the only time a player wasn't happy and ran behind my back to management to complain. I could have swallowed my pride a bit and tried to talk to Jason and work things out, but in those days I was very stubborn. I wasn't a my-way-or-the-highway type of coach, but I was stubborn when it came to going to a player like that and saying, "Hey, man, we've got to talk." My pride wouldn't allow me to do that.

We had been to the Finals two years in a row and we had the same personnel, so had we stuck together I think we could have won a championship. It's something I should have fought harder for, but instead we parted ways, and assistant coach Lawrence Frank took over.

The assistant coaches are the players' friends. That's always how it is. If players want a change, they usually want their friend to step in. So I wished him well as I went on my way. If I hire someone and he gets a head coaching job, then that reflects well on me. If a person comes from my system and does well, then we all look good. When you delegate authority properly, not only do you build a winning team, but you can also create a culture that can spread throughout the league.

CHARLIE: PROVIDING OPTIONS

You can never be worried that somebody's going to take your job. In fact, you want to surround yourself with people who *can* take your job, and you want them to make you better. When you trust that they're putting the best interests of the company first, and they believe you trust them, then they're going to work more to help you.

Every good boss I've had has given me space to make my own decisions and my own mistakes. No one ever tried to slow my progress because they feared my personal success.

When I was working with Bob Bolingbroke and I had a point of view but wasn't sure if it was the right point of view, I would sit with him and ask him what he thought. He'd ask me the pros and cons and provide options for the future. He was never somebody who would say, "I insist that you do A, B, C, D." It would be, "Here's what I see," and we would discuss it before making a joint decision. He provided various choices and left it to me to be the decision maker. That to me is good leadership, and it's something I've tried to do as both a CEO and a chairman of the board.

To have the courage of your own convictions is not something that somebody can necessarily teach you. It builds over time, starting with how you were raised. You have to know that you're good at what you do, and if something goes wrong, it can't break down that conviction.

As a leader you want the team working with you to have confidence in themselves and to know that the CEO has confidence in them. You give them the tools to succeed and trust that they will succeed.

Giving them the tools is essentially your job as a leader. I've always felt that the more people know about what is going on in an organization, and the more access they have to the data they need to make the best decisions, the better they will do. I never felt it was good to hold in any information when the data could lead to better decisions.

At Deer Park and McKesson Water we improved our data systems on every level, from marketing to sales, productivity, and financial results. Whenever we got new information we shared it with the entire company. We said, "Here are the numbers, take this information and do your job to the best of your ability." We were far more successful that way than we would have been if we had kept the data among the top executives and just told everyone what to do every day.

Even with Freshpet, I think people like and respect me as a board member because I'm not trying to do their jobs. I'm trying to think about what else is needed to make the company better. Just as when I was a CEO, I'm trying to get people very comfortable handling a job on their own. I'm not in their hair every day, but when I have an idea I'm sharing the idea and talking about it. I'm giving the team every piece of information I have, and one day, if they have my job, then I know I did my job the right way.

X's and O's

- Delegate authority and let partnerships/mentor situations happen naturally instead of forcing them on the team.

- When the job isn't done correctly, encourage others to rethink their approach instead of fixing everything for them.

- Success is achieved through team chemistry and everyone working toward the same goal.

- Don't fear the success of others, but rather encourage those around you to aim for leadership roles.

Chapter 13

Ego versus Respect

"Part of me suspects that I'm a loser and the other part of me thinks I'm God Almighty." —John Lennon

Core values exist within a true leader, but the battle between confidence and overconfidence often lies in the respect a leader has for others. Be the best you and trust that those around you are committed to victory.

BYRON: SUCCESS IS EARNED

When I got the job as the head coach of the then–New Orleans Hornets, I thought, *I got this*. I had won championships as a player and taken the Nets to the Finals twice as a head coach, so I was confident I could take a team from any situation and turn them into winners.

There's a big difference between confidence and ego. I'm a confident man, but I never let any past success make me feel I deserve something or I'm owed something. That mentality never works, especially in the NBA, where the phrase *Let's make a change* is heard the instant times get tough.

Between sports media and social media, every year there are more voices out there saying, "Let's make a change," and eventually ownership starts to listen. There's pressure on management to get somebody different instead of letting somebody get better. It doesn't matter that you took a team to the Finals one year if you don't do it again the next year.

That uncertainty in the job market helps quell the ego, but with players it's a different story. A lot of guys come in having been the best player in high school and college and any other league or tournament they've played in prior to the NBA. They get drafted to a team and plan for a twenty-year career. Their ego is through the roof.

I had a player in New Jersey I had to pull to the side and talk to about life after basketball. When he signed with the team, he bought a house in New York and a house in Las Vegas, two Escalades, and a bunch of other toys. I looked at him and I said, "Son, you just signed a three-year deal with a fourth-year option that's a team option. Your contract is worth a total of probably $1.8 million. You just spent that in less than a couple of months."

His answer to me: "Well, I'll sign another contract."

I tried to sit down with him and talk to him about injuries and the number of other circumstances that might make his plan go awry, but he didn't get it. After that third year, the team didn't pick up his option, and he went to play overseas for significantly less money.

In New Orleans I really wanted to put together a team of quality guys. You can have a big ego, but then you've got to be really good. I mean really good. Hall of Fame, top-fifty-of-all-time good—or else things will eventually go very bad. I think that's always the case, but especially with me; since I don't put up with that stuff, a big ego will lead to a big disaster.

My first year we had quality guys like David West, P. J. Brown, Baron Davis, and Jamaal Magloire, but we needed more talent around them, so we won only eighteen games. We drafted J. R. Smith, but he wasn't mature enough for our system at the time, so he lasted only a couple of seasons.

In the 2005 NBA draft that summer we got lucky. There's really no other way to describe it. Our GM, Jeff Bower, went down to Wake Forest to watch Chris Paul practice and play and to meet his parents. He spent a whole week there, and when he left he was big-time impressed. He told us even before we brought Chris Paul in for the workout that he thought the kid would be special. After the workout we all agreed he was the best player in the draft. We had the fourth pick, and when Paul fell to us we were in heaven. He was not only a huge talent but also a quality guy, so I knew we were about to turn a corner.

CHARLIE: QUALITY CONTROL IS NOT A SCIENCE

There really isn't a pattern when it comes to hiring the right person. It's easy to say you want someone with the perfect balance of confidence and respect, but everyone reacts differently to adversity, and sometimes ego gets in the way.

When you are running a large company it's sometimes hard to know what people are thinking. Some will say one thing to your face when they're saying the complete opposite behind your back. Then you hear about it and you can't believe it. Other people are honest and say, "I'm not comfortable with this kind of change," and then you work out a separation that's in the best interests of both that person and the organization. Either way, making a personnel change is necessary.

After the consolidation at McKesson Water, some of the vice presidents of the strategic business units were moved to more functional roles within the company. In my eyes their new jobs were actually more important, but not everyone saw it that way.

There was one person who went from running a strategic business unit that had maybe 75,000 customers in total to being the head of all operations with 750,000 customers on his watch. Where I come from that's a promotion, but this guy liked the autonomy of managing all functions within the strategic business unit. He ran everything for that smaller customer base, and to him that was the better job.

He didn't realize how important the new role was, and there was nothing I could do to convince him that his new role was far more important than his previous one. In fact, it was the biggest job in the company, but he couldn't wrap his arms around it. He didn't understand it and he couldn't embrace it.

At the end of the day, I think he wanted my job. He looked around at my executive team and me and didn't respect what we were trying to do. He wanted to be the president, coach, and star player all by himself.

If someone below ultimately feels that they should have someone else's job, it's up to the overall boss of that manager to determine whether the manager is doing the right job and improving with coaching. If despite their ego issues they are still doing a good job, you can simply tell the employee that you like what they're doing, but that unfortunately there is no upward mobility right now for them. Then it is up to that person to decide what they want to do with their future.

If I saw someone who was ready for more but we weren't able to give it to them, then I had no problem telling them to look outside the company. We had a second-level manager in finance who was really an up-and-comer. We actually supported him in getting his master's degree, and then he got a great offer somewhere else, and we told him he should take it. He eventually came back to us at a higher level some time later, because he'd burned no bridges. He stayed in touch with the people who were heading the finance group, and when we had an opening at a higher level he got the job.

As for the other guy—the guy who wanted my job—well, that was a different story. He was disgruntled and it affected his performance. Ultimately you want all your people to earn as much as they can and grow as much as they can, but when someone's ego stands in the way of that success, then it's time for them to go. We made a change and moved him out of the company, and were better off for it. Hopefully he was too.

BYRON: A PERFECT MIX OF CONFIDENCE AND CLASS

That first season with Chris Paul got off to a rough start since Hurricane Katrina forced our team to move to Oklahoma City. The fans there were incredible, but with everyone being removed from their homes, it felt as if every game was still a road game.

Chris Paul was a stud from day one, though. He was just nineteen years old when we drafted him, and that summer I gave him a video playbook. A week or so after the draft, Summer League started, and when we played our first Summer League game I said, "All right, CP, we're going to run chin, so you start here—" And I started to explain it to him, but he cut me off.

"I got it, Coach."

"What do you mean you got it?"

"I went through the video playbook you gave me," he said. "I got it."

"All right," I said skeptically. "Well, show me."

I called out a few plays and he had it. He knew everything. I couldn't believe it. I turned to one of my assistant coaches and said, "We got something special. This kid is going to be special."

Throughout that first season, he lived up to the standard he'd set from day one. He worked hard in practice and all the guys followed his lead. He was always champing at the bit to get going in practice, and he trusted the coaching staff with every decision we made.

Having a guy like Chris Paul in your corner is important to successful coaching. In the locker room, when the guys police each other, I don't have to watch every single move. Paul's leadership and lack of ego allowed him to keep that locker room straightened out so that when it was game time, they were ready. It took one thing off my plate and I could focus on strategy.

Everything he did was done with a certain level of respect. There was a game when we had the ball with a few seconds left, down by a point, and obviously Chris wanted the ball, because all champions do. But he didn't want to show up any of the other players on the team, so he casually walked by me and whispered, "Give me the ball."

He didn't want to be the guy in the huddle demanding the ball, but he believed in himself enough to take the big shots. I had never seen anything like it, but I was impressed. I drew up the play for him, and sure enough he hit the shot.

There were times early on when it went a little overboard. Once P. J. Brown was going in the wrong direction on a certain play, and I turned to Chris to help make the adjustment.

"Look, you've got to tell him to get over here," I said.

"Coach, he's been in the league ten years, I can't tell him."

"But they look up to you," I said. "They look to you for direction.

So even though you're only nineteen years old, these guys have watched you in training camp, they have nothing but respect for you. You have to lead them on the court. So if he's not where he's supposed to be, you've got to tell them. And believe me, they'll respond to you."

He trusted me as the coach and became more vocal. They knew he was the leader of this team, but it took maybe half a season for him to realize it. By the end of the season he was rookie of the year and a leader of a team that was about to do great things.

CHARLIE: EARLY INFLUENCES

A lot of that mentality you see from a guy like Chris Paul comes from the way he was raised. Some people rise to the occasion when they're forced into leadership situations or put in the position to lead. Harry Truman was never much of a leader, but he did really great things as president. But for many people like Paul, that level of respect mixed with work ethic and lack of ego is something that was ingrained from childhood.

Having grown up in Poland during the Depression, my father was a really hard worker who left the country in 1937. Virtually all of his family was wiped out soon after that in the Holocaust.

He met my mother when he was living in Denmark, studying for his PhD at the University of Copenhagen. They applied for resident permits in the United States, where my mother was, and Denmark, where my dad was, and they agreed that whichever came through first, that's where they'd live. It was good fortune that brought them to America during a horrible time in European history.

Throughout his adult life in this country, my dad felt that as a father his most important responsibility was to make enough money so that his family could live in a good house, always have food on the table, and take the occasional vacation, and that his kids could go to college. He didn't have time to be around for us very much. When he got home, he'd be so tired that he'd sit down and fall asleep watching television.

As a businessman he was very much a socialist who believed in the sharing of wealth with the worker, even though he grew up in a wealthy family in Poland. That socialist attitude was there throughout his career in many ways. As he worked his way up in the supermarket industry in the United States, he was always fighting for the people who worked for him and was always having troubles with the people above him.

The people he reported to felt he was looking out for the employees rather than the company as a whole, but he believed that if the frontline people were on his side, the company would benefit. He had a great relationship with the unions and with his people. When he moved jobs, everyone wanted to go with him. They knew that not only was he really smart, he had their backs, so people would run through walls for him.

He never presented with notes or had a written speech, because to him, if you're reading a prepared speech then you're not talking to the audience. His belief was that you have to engage the people you're talking to every step of the way. He was brilliant at weaving a story and delivering a punch line in a way that people really understood.

I watched the way he handled people and how he respected the workers, and his example was instilled in me well before I entered the workforce. He always told me he'd support my education and help me where he could, but I had to build my career on my own. From my first job to every business venture that followed, his influence was there, and I think I'm a better leader for it.

BYRON: CHARACTER CREATES CHAMPIONS

Every player has an ego. Great players know they are great. But guys like Chris Paul balance ego with respect for those who came before them and a trust in the coaching staff to do our jobs. That's what separates the talented from the leaders.

Charlie is right: a lot of it has to do with the way a person is raised. My parents raised me to be an honest hard worker, and taught me that everything in life must be earned. I had chores at home until I left for college. I cleaned the kitchen and washed the dishes, and we didn't have a sprinkler system, so I was out there once a week watering the grass.

In college I let my grades slip, so I figured I could go home for a few months and then just throw my name into the NBA draft.

"You ain't staying here," Mom shouted when I walked in the door. "My son ain't no quitter. Take your butt back to school and go to class."

I got in the car and went back to school. I apologized to my coaches and apologized to each teacher, and focused on my education.

CP was raised in a similar type of family. He worked hard and respected the game and the leaders around him, because he understood that everyone has to do their job in order for the team to win.

What made us so great in LA was that while everybody knew that Magic Johnson was the leader of the team, he would never say it publicly or even privately with us, because of Kareem. He would bark out this and that and yell to get here and there, but had so much respect for the captain that he wouldn't step on his toes. When we would get into fights—and back in those days there were a lot of them—Kareem would be over on the other side relaxing while Magic, Coop, and I would all be in the middle of it. That was his style and we respected it. Once Cap left, Magic was known more publicly as the leader, and he became the captain.

But the thing that I loved about him was that even then, he had no problem taking some direction when *he* wasn't where he was supposed to be. He was a leader but wasn't a do-as-I-say guy. If he wasn't doing his job that day, he wanted the criticism. He led in a way that made us comfortable enough to say, "Hey, Magic, get your butt over here, where you're supposed to be."

Chris Paul was the same way. He was always learning, always growing. He treated practice as if it were as important as a game, and that mind-set trickled down to the other players. He respected everyone and was a leader whom everyone respected.

Before CP's third season I knew we had clicked as a team. When the schedule came out, I even told Mayor Ray Nagin that we would win between fifty-two and fifty-six games. I was confident that we had a team that could have one of the best records in the league. We were going to be able to compete with everybody. We won fifty-six games and made it to the Conference Semifinals. Our disadvantage against teams like the Lakers and Spurs was that we had no prior experience at that level. Those two teams had won championships, so they had experience. If ownership had kept the team together for three more years, I think we would have broken through and made it to an NBA Finals. But this year was a turning point for the organization. I won Coach of the Year, and Chris Paul established himself as one of the best players in the league. It all started that first season, though, when he showed up respecting the game instead of shouting about all the respect he deserved.

CHARLIE: NEGOTIATING EGO

Plenty of times during a negotiation the egos come out in full force. People inflate the worth of their product or service, and their pride won't allow them to drop a penny below a predetermined number.

Back when I was buying up water companies I went out to Las Vegas to buy a family business from a guy who was a very good person, but also very Las Vegas. We negotiated back and forth and got stuck at a $10,000 difference between our estimates of the value of the company. The total purchase price was somewhere around $2.5 million, so concerning yourself with a $10,000 difference is just silly. At some point you're arguing just out of pride, because one way or the other, it's not going to make or break a deal. You're just trying to win for the sake of winning.

To settle all of this, I decided to speak his language. "I tell you what," I said. "We'll play one hand of liar's poker. If you win, we'll pay ten thousand dollars more. If I win, we'll pay ten thousand dollars less."

He was up for the gamble, but I actually won the hand. I was very lucky on that one. A lot of deals get blown because pride and ego get in the way. Because we were able to have a little fun with it, the guy felt as if he'd lost a card game and not a business deal. Afterward we laughed about it, and went out and had a good dinner that I'm sure I paid for.

When it comes to dealing with egos, you have to be more prepared than the person you're negotiating with. You need to know what is acceptable to you and what isn't. If you get everybody you have to get approval from committed to a specific number, you can be totally honest about it. You can say, "Here's my drop-dead number. I can't go beyond that."

If you can get a deal done at that number, that's great. If it's not what the other party wants, you have to try to find other ways that you can make up the difference so everyone walks away a winner.

That's always my goal. I want to make it a win-win. I tell the other party to tell me what's most important, and I do my best to make it work. In some deals you use your stock to buy a company. Other times you might do it with cash. Sometimes you're just buying assets, and other times you're buying the whole corporation.

If you just buy assets, then the taxes are higher on the seller than if he sells the whole corporation. Sometimes the question isn't how much money a person is getting but when they are getting it. I might not be able to give you $1 million today. I don't have it in the bank. But I can give you $200,000 today and once a year over the next four years, along with the interest associated with it, to give you the same value as if all the money had been given to you on day one.

There are ways to find solutions that meet both that person's and the company's needs. But when their needs boil down to a mere ego boost, sometimes you have to just roll the dice and gamble on taking on that ego directly.

X's and O's

- Be the best at the job you have and you'll eventually get the job you want.

- Individual success comes from the perfect mix of confidence and respect.

- Once you understand how the person across the table from you thinks, you can negotiate nearly any outcome.

- Let the best idea win, whether it is yours or not.

Chapter 14

Working with Your Strengths

"The first requisite for success is to develop the ability to focus and apply your physical and mental energies to the problem at hand without growing weary." —Thomas Edison

When you want to get better it's human nature to reach beyond your natural abilities, but true success comes when you make the most of what you've got rather than trying to be someone you're not.

BYRON: FINDING THE ALL-STAR WITHIN

When you're a coach, you're constantly trying to get the most out of your players. The challenge is getting all fifteen guys to be the best versions of themselves for an entire season. That's what wins championships—every guy on the team having his best season.

Sometimes, though, you can push a guy in the wrong direction, by not working within his skill set. I had Tyson Chandler playing for me in New Orleans, and he was the best center I've coached. He was terrific and a leader on the team, and he very badly wanted to be an all-star. He had the numbers in his first season with the team—averaging ten points, twelve rebounds, and a couple of blocked shots per game. Those numbers are all-star-worthy for a center, but he wasn't getting that call.

He came to me one day and said, "Coach, I want to be an all-star next season. How do I get there?"

"Maybe we have to throw the ball to you a little bit more, maybe you have to score a little bit more," I said. "Or maybe it's because it's the first year that you've had this type of season. Maybe you have to duplicate your results next year to gain that stature."

I liked him a lot, so I really wanted him to get there. We came to the conclusion that over the summer he'd work on his post game, and the next season I'd try to feature him more on offense.

The next season, the 2007–08 season, we threw him the ball a lot more than we had in the previous year. But we were getting away from our plan, and I knew it was probably a mistake. I just wanted it so badly for him.

To his credit, the guy knew who he was. He came to me about twenty-five games into the season with a change of plans.

"You know what, Coach," he said. "That's not me, I'm a defender, I'm a rebounder, and I'm a shot blocker. I'm a defensive player. I'm not a post-up guy. I just gotta be me."

I actually felt relieved that he'd said it first. When a guy works hard and is such a strong player, you want the best for him, but the team comes first and he knew it. That's what made him special. I might have gone until the all-star break playing a style of basketball that saw Tyson getting the ball more on offense in order to see if he could make it. That would have been a bad coaching move on my part. Instead he knew himself, he knew the team, and he made the call to put the organization first.

When we switched back to his comfort zone, he played that role to a T with our team. He was our best communicator on the defensive end, and he erased a whole lot of defensive mistakes that other players made. And you know what, five years later, being himself paid off when he made the all-star team as a member of the New York Knicks. His numbers were even a few points lower than in those first two seasons in New Orleans, but he was Tyson Chandler, a dominant center for thirteen years at that point, and he deserved it.

CHARLIE: YOU CAN'T FORCE GREATNESS

When you try to change what works in hopes of hitting it big, odds are it will be a misstep. Normally I bet on the jockey and not the horse, but when I was introduced to the Piloti group through another investor I thought the concept was really intriguing, so I went against my usual investing approach.

The concept behind this company, which made shoes for race car drivers and race car enthusiasts, was exciting because it targeted a huge market. The product line went from serious shoes for race car drivers all the way down to casual, sporty shoes for fans of NASCAR, Indy racing, and the like. Even the ones for fans had a rounded heel that made it easier to switch between gas and brake.

I loved the concept and invested in the company even though the couple who'd started it had no experience running a business. The husband had been a designer of shoes in that industry and his wife worked side by side with him, but neither of them had ever run anything.

The shoes were great quality and I felt there was certainly a market for such a product, but the problem was that the husband was not an experienced leader. His focus was too spread out and we never got traction in any segment of that field. He was trying to be everything to everybody. He was participating in tent shows and he was trying to get into the Nordstroms of the world and the mass shoe outlets, so we were not successful in any of those areas because we weren't uniquely focused on one.

The founder burned through a lot of money far too quickly, and by the time we realized we had to find a replacement, we had lost too much money to reinvest. We couldn't hire a top-notch person without having commitments to fund the company, and I thought we were going to throw good money after bad, so we decided to essentially shut the company down.

I fell in love with the concept and went against my rule. That was my mistake. The founder did not have a track record of successfully running anything, but I thought that I could mentor him and show him how to apply more focus in his direction and leadership. It got to a point where I just exploded in a board meeting and told them I was done. Looking back, that was an embarrassing moment. That's when we shut down. We stopped funding.

It was my worst personal effort as well as my worst investment. But it was a lesson learned. Sometimes you actually can't teach an old dog new tricks. Sometimes you can't teach a dog of any age much of anything. As a leader you have to try to bring out the best in people, but know their limits and work with the skills they have. As an investor, it's best to stick to your plan and not try to force someone into a role they are not comfortable in.

BYRON: WINNING WITHOUT YOUR LEADER

As a coach you dream of landing a job where you are coaching a superstar surrounded by a few all-stars and other players who know exactly who they are and what their role is. That perfect combination is a big part of success, but often if a team is looking for a new coach they don't have any of those things.

After my time with New Orleans was up, the next opportunity presented to me was with the Cleveland Cavaliers. They had fired Mike Brown after a season in which LeBron James won the MVP but the team underachieved and lost to the Boston Celtics in the Eastern Conference Semifinals.

LeBron was about to become a free agent and there were rumors that he might leave. With him I had a legitimate shot at coaching a team to a championship. Without him I'd be starting over.

I thought about the job at hand and decided that it was a win-win situation for me. If LeBron came back we were in great shape, and if he didn't I would have the opportunity to rebuild this team into something great. I pride myself on being able to mold young players and help them achieve greatness, and after what I was able to do in New Orleans I was confident I could do it in Cleveland.

Going into it, ownership really didn't think LeBron was going to leave. Part of the reason they wanted to hire me may have been my relationship with Chris Paul. They were trying to lure him over to the Cavs to join forces with LeBron, and since I had coached Paul in New Orleans, they saw me as a perfect fit to coach the team.

That's what they were thinking. I was thinking, *Either way I'm good.*

On July 1, the same day LeBron James officially became an unrestricted free agent, I officially accepted the job as head coach of the Cleveland Cavaliers. After I took the job I was sitting with Chris Grant, general manager of the Cavs at the time, and we were planning for the upcoming season and talking about LeBron.

"You know what?" I said. "Let me call one of my guys who knows him well and find out if he's coming back or not."

This was about four days before "the Decision," and I called up a very good friend of LeBron's and he said, "Coach, let me get back to you." Ten minutes later he called me back and broke the news.

"He's gone."

I told Chris Grant that my sources had told me he was leaving, but Grant didn't believe it. No one in the organization wanted to believe it. No one in the state of Ohio wanted to believe it. They really felt that he wouldn't leave, so they weren't prepared for it.

The night of the Decision,—July 8, 2010—we had just finished working out a group of guys for our Summer League team. I was in my office ranking the twenty or so guys that we'd invited in to work out to see if we would take any of them to Las Vegas for the Summer League. Like everyone else in America, I turned on ESPN to watch the big show, and LeBron came on and said the famous words, "I'm taking my talents to South Beach."

OK, I guess my guy was right, I thought as I turned the TV off, and I went back to ranking the rest of the guys. Then I got in my car and forgot all about it. That's just how my mind works. There's no need to dwell on bad news.

At that particular time, I was staying at the Ritz-Carlton downtown, and as I was driving back to my hotel all hell was breaking loose. People were burning jerseys. The big "Witness" photo on the side of a downtown Cleveland office building was already halfway down. It was madness.

Even though I had been prepared for the news, it was still tough. One day management is telling me that I might be coaching LeBron and Chris Paul, and the next day the whole city is crushed. As the head coach, I tried to keep an even keel as much as possible, but internally I'd been tossing and turning because I knew I had an opportunity. When it fell through, I knew right away that I was going to be starting from the bottom.

Once LeBron left I had to change my perspective on what the season was going to look like and on what our roster would look like. I had to work with what I had. The philosophy and work ethic stayed the same, but now I was building from the ground up, so the timetable for success changed.

I remained positive throughout, but owner Dan Gilbert did not. His letter publicly bashing LeBron was tough for me to read because it showed a different side of Dan Gilbert from what I'd seen in the meetings that led up to the night of the Decision. It was a personal attack on LeBron, who for the record had every right to leave. That's why they call it free agency. I thought the way he had done it was wrong, but that didn't change the outcome. That didn't change the fact that he was no longer on the team.

Gilbert's letter set my tenure with the Cavs off to a bad start. It wasn't the attitude I had hoped for. I didn't want to look back. I wanted to have a positive attitude and move forward. Once LeBron left we had to move on. We wanted to be successful, and in order for that to happen, we had to turn the men on the roster into winners. The easiest way to win is to make sure tomorrow is better than today, and after those first few weeks in the summer, it was obvious that there was nowhere to go but up.

CHARLIE: BETTING ON POTENTIAL

Just as when LeBron left Cleveland, we were missing that leadership presence on the executive board at Piloti. Finding the next man up can be tough, especially when you look around and can't find someone who has been there before.

After Clorox bought Deer Park, I put in my allotted time and made the decision to move to McKesson. Before we parted ways, the company asked me to recommend my replacement. There was a fellow who had been in the bottled water industry for many, many years. He was an accountant by training and had run a large home and office water business on the East Coast. Late in his career he had come to work with us, and he was well liked among his peers.

There was also an up-and-coming guy running our marketing who was a traditional consumer packaged goods marketer. He was young and aggressive, but maybe a bit immature at that point, I thought.

Thinking more in terms of who would get along better with the management at Clorox, I recommended the older fellow. I just thought that the younger person needed a little more seasoning, and the guy with more years under his belt would be a better transition person for the job. I thought more about keeping things calm and status quo for the next few years, instead of focusing on innovation and taking the company to the next level. I thought this guy could carry the torch and then maybe the young marketing wiz could take over a few years down the line.

What I missed in the whole process was the politics at Clorox. As it turned out, there was a change in senior leadership at the company, and they didn't feel that the water business was the place to be. The guy I recommended was not the right guy to be selling top executives on why the company was going to be successful. In hindsight they would've gotten much more forward thinking from the younger person, and it might just have influenced them to keep the business.

Maturity comes in different ways. It's one thing to give a person more responsibility and let them make their mistakes. It's another thing to have that person become the head coach when they are still on a steep learning curve. The question becomes, Do you take a less experienced person and have him run the whole company, or hire someone who has a lot more experience? That's a real trade-off.

In this case, since senior management decided it wasn't a business they wanted to be in, in retrospect I should have taken the risk of promoting the younger guy for the job. If I had been wise about it, I would have rolled the dice and taken the risk, because in reality I had been that guy ten years earlier. He had the skill set and the drive to do the job, but I just thought he needed some more tread on the tires. When the talent is there, though, you should use it as soon as possible.

BYRON: MAKING SUCCESSFUL ADJUSTMENTS

One of the guys I had in Cleveland was Tristan Thompson, who we knew would be a real workhorse. He'd do all the dirty work and would be a pivotal team player. He didn't have the talent to be an all-star-type player, but he had the desire to be exactly what we needed for that team—a hell of a defender, a rebounder, and a shot blocker. Those are the kind of things that lead to long careers in the NBA, and any player should be proud of them.

Most of these guys, when they get in the league, the first two years they probably still think they can be an all-star. They always think they're better than they are. Tristan was drafted fourth overall, so expectations were high, but the quicker a player like him can realize what he needs to do to be successful in this league, the better off he will be. It's better for the team too. He figured it out quickly, and I think he's going to be a very good player in this league for a long time.

Tristan's problem was that he was a terrible free throw shooter with no post moves. If he got the ball under the basket and he was going up for a dunk, everybody fouled him. He was a little bit like Dwight Howard; you can kill Dwight's game by putting him on the free throw line.

But we found a way to fix it. In the middle of his rookie season we discovered that Tristan was really more of a right-hand player. He shot his free throws with his left hand, but everything else he did was right-hand dominant.

With thirty games left in the season, I made a choice to try to get him to be a right-hand shooter. In practice we had him shoot free throws with his left hand and with his right hand. The free throws with his right hand were so much more fluid. Then we gave him a football; he could barely throw the ball with his left hand, while with his right he threw a tight spiral.

The whole coaching staff looked at each other in amazement. How had he been shooting lefty all those years?

What made him successful was that he was willing to make changes in his game to be a better basketball player. When I talk about working within your skill set, I should say the key component is *knowing* your skill set. A guy like Tyson Chandler was trying to do too much and stepping out of his element in an attempt to score more points. That wasn't good. But a guy like Tristan Thompson needed that change to discover his true skills. It works both ways, but once you have it figured out, you have to be the best version of yourself night in and night out in order to win ball games.

CHARLIE: LEARNING FROM MISTAKES

When I invested in Freshpet and took on the role of chairman of the board, I brought all these past scenarios with me. The concept of working with what you have definitely rings true when you are dealing with a start-up, but regardless of what prior business knowledge you bring to the table, you'll inevitably have to deal with shortcomings.

When we started out at Freshpet we had a much smaller team than we all probably would have liked, but that's what the finances dictated. It forced us to all become jacks-of-all-trades, but in the process we made some big, expensive errors.

As an organization we made a decision that we were going to be a pet food company and not a refrigeration company. We wanted to make great pet food, but we did not want to own the refrigerators. A year and a half in, we started to realize that if we didn't buy the refrigerators, very few of the retailers were going to buy them for us. We had this great pet food but no way to get it to consumers, so we had to bite the bullet and buy the fridges.

We were a bunch of guys who knew how to make pet food, market it, sell it, and operate a pet food company, but we didn't know anything about refrigerators. We put one of the team members in charge of the refrigerators, but he didn't know any more about it than any of us. Before we knew it we had about a hundred fridges out there that weren't holding temperature. When that happens, the food goes bad.

When we fixed that problem they started leaking and causing a potential hazard because customers could fall on the wet floors. Eventually the refrigerators started breaking down altogether at an alarming rate. When the refrigerators were leaking, that was really bad. When they started breaking down, it could easily have been game over.

Picture what these fridges looked like when the lights started going out and they became just big dark boxes in the stores that didn't even keep the food at the proper temperature. At the time it felt like a disaster.

At first, to fix this problem and keep these stores selling our product, we went out into the field and rebuilt these fridges one by one. In the early stages of a company you don't have the resources to work with a big refrigeration company or hire a consultant to figure this out, so you just go and do it. We all learned way more about the inner workings of the grocery store refrigerator than we'd ever expected to learn.

We were able to keep it together, and eventually we ended up hiring outside people to get the job done. But in the beginning it was just us going from store to store trying to fix these things.

It gave all of us an appreciation for the difficulty of this aspect of the company. It taught us a lesson about the respect that we needed to have and the skill we needed to bring into the organization to handle the refrigeration part of the business. We couldn't just take a sales and marketing guy and give him the responsibility of running a portion of the business he had never run before. We needed to develop some competency in refrigeration first, and then make decisions.

A company like Pepsi or Coca-Cola has a whole department dedicated to refrigerators and has been doing it for many years. We just knew we needed refrigerators, so we went out and bought some. The reality is that not all fridges are created equal, and in some regards we did the equivalent of putting household units into retail stores.

Mistakes will get made, and I like to think I was able to keep the team calm in the face of adversity. This was in the early stages of the company's growth, so we were able to survive. Had it been in a later stage it would have been a large and expensive mistake that might have done irreversible damage to the company. If it had been a thousand-store rollout with Walmart or Target, they would have told us to get the refrigerators out of there as soon as they weren't holding temperature. If people were slipping and falling there could have been tons of lawsuits.

But we lucked out in a sense and were able to right the ship. We all became a little smarter on the subject, and, most importantly, we didn't forget the lesson learned. As a leader you have to make sure to build these lessons into the DNA of the company, especially at a place like Freshpet, where we didn't have the time or money to make the same mistakes twice.

X's and O's

- Put the team first and you'll ultimately be the best version of you.

- Bet on the jockey, not the horse.

- Take a risk on rising talent instead of promoting a leader who has simply put in his or her time.

- Determine the core competencies needed to be successful and strengthen them.

Chapter 15

Sticking to Your Guns

"Get up, stand up, don't give up the fight." —Bob Marley

On the road to success, people will fight you every step of the way. Sometimes what's good for one part of the team isn't what's good for everyone else involved. The only way to be a winner is to stick to your guns and fight tooth and nail for what you believe is right.

BYRON: PLAY TO WIN

When you are the coach, you aren't the boss of the organization. There is a GM and/or a president and, of course, the team owner; they call the shots and are above you in the pecking order. But when you're hired as a coach, they are giving you the keys to make the decisions necessary to win basketball games.

That's why you'll never hear a respectable coach talk about tanking. Obviously the numbers don't lie, and a team well out of playoff contention may do better in the lottery if it continues to lose games, but coaches want to go out and win every game regardless of what the future holds. It's in our blood.

Players are going to follow the cue of the coach. If they think that you're tanking, then you lose credibility and all respect, and they give up. If that happens, they can probably never play for you again.

In Cleveland we tried to win as many games as possible. When we started losing, and losing a lot, my thought process was never to look at the clock, sub guys in and out, and try to lose the basketball game. Do I want a good pick in the draft? Of course I do. But I want to win this game I'm coaching more.

Sometimes, for a GM or owner, it's not about tanking but about selling tickets. That is their job, after all. But I'm sticking to winning no matter what anyone tells me, and if that means losing my job, then so be it.

When I was with the Hornets, Chris "Birdman" Andersen was a popular player. He was suspended for violating the NBA drug policy and missed two years of playing time. When he returned toward the end of the 2007–08 season, team owner George Shinn wanted me to play him right away. We were a team on our way to fifty-six wins and first in our division that season, and they wanted to shake things up because Birdman was a crowd favorite.

I, of course, said no, which upset ownership. In the beginning of the 2009–10 season it was more of the same. We drafted Darren Collison, a guard out of UCLA, and acquired rookie Marcus Thornton that year. Early on, Bower was watching every practice and sending me messages.

"Shinn wants you to play the rookies," he said.

"They're not ready," I replied. "When they're ready I'll play them."

He came to me and told me a second time, and I said, "Look, if he wants to play them, he can coach them."

And so, nine games into the season, I was let go. But I didn't lose sleep over it, because I knew I had done the right thing. Shinn probably wanted to see what these guys could do because he planned to trade away some of our stars in order to save money. He wanted to take minutes away from Chris Paul and Mo Peterson to see how these rookies would perform. That just wasn't going to work for me.

Jeff Bower took over as coach, and slowly they started trading away the best players on the team. They finished with thirty-seven wins—last in the division—and didn't make the playoffs. If that was what they wanted, it wasn't something I could have been part of anyway.

As a leader you always have to follow your gut and do what you think is best to help the team win. I would put my mom out there if I thought it would give us a chance to win basketball games. I have no agenda. I want to put the best product on the floor to give me an opportunity to win games, and that was our plan. Shinn saw the team from a business standpoint: put people in the seats and try to make as much money as possible. In my mind, winning games puts people in the seats too, so I'm going to try to win and I'm going to trust my instincts and play the best players. I lost my job in the process, but I kept my integrity.

CHARLIE: FIGHTING GOLIATH

When dealing with other investors—especially ones that are large companies—you're going to have to respond to their direction and demands in a way you might not have to with individual investors or small investor groups. Just as the GM and the owner of a basketball team might have different goals from a coach, a large company partner will also have different views of success.

Tyson Foods, which at the outset provided Freshpet with various services, became our first strategic investor when we needed more funding. At the outset it was a good relationship that made sense for both parties. The CEO of Tyson, who had approved the investment in Freshpet, had wanted to get out from under being just a commodities business. For Tyson we were a natural fit, because it could provide a lot of raw materials to us. It had a global refrigerated distribution business, and we were anything but a commodity.

Then the CEO ended up getting fired. The person who replaced him was a commodities guy who was not comfortable with a start-up business that might not be hitting its numbers from quarter to quarter.

There was inconsistency in our performance, which is typical for a start-up, but it wasn't something the new CEO could handle. Eventually he told the people from Tyson who were directly involved in our business that he wanted Tyson to control Freshpet. He thought our lack of consistency was a product of management's not knowing what it was doing.

This CEO instructed his lieutenants to tell me to fire the top people and move the business to Arkansas so Tyson and its management team could run it. My response at the time was, "You're out of your minds. I'm not going to do that. What in the world are you thinking?"

The point is that the CEO wasn't thinking. He didn't care about the growth of our business or want to take the time to learn the ins and outs of a start-up like ours. He just saw numbers and inconsistency and thought that if the numbers were going to fluctuate it was going to happen on his terms.

Under this CEO, Freshpet just wasn't the business for Tyson anymore, but I sure as hell wasn't going to let the company ruin it for the rest of us. I'd believed in Freshpet from day one, and I trusted our management team because I saw them work, listened to their plans, and knew that they had what it takes to win. In this case it was my job to step up and remind the folks at Tyson that the rest of us were not giving up.

BYRON: DEVELOPING TOUGHNESS

A leader has to be tough. You have to stand up for what you believe in, and you have to have thick skin. If you go home and cry every time you lose a game or even a job, you're not going to survive in this business—or, likely, in any business, for that matter.

For me I think that toughness started developing at a young age. When I was a kid, my brother was always getting into trouble. We didn't get along too well, but he was my younger brother so I was always there to protect him.

One day he came home with a black eye instead of some money he'd won gambling. A guy a year older than I (and three years older than my brother) had cheated him out of the money and punched him in the face for good measure.

"Where's this guy at?" I said when I heard the story. "Let's go."

We went over there with a friend of mine and confronted the guy.

"I didn't come over here to start any trouble, but my brother here says you owe him some money," I said, looking the guy dead in the eye. "Give him his money."

He basically told me where I could shove it, but I said we weren't leaving without the money. I was friendly with this guy's sister so I had been at this house before. It wasn't a dangerous situation in my mind, but then the kid came back with a gun and things changed.

He pointed the gun directly in my face and told me to leave, but my friend grabbed his arm and wrestled it away from him. We all left unscathed, but that was a pretty scary situation. There are times when backing down might be a good idea, and this was one of them. There's no need to put your life in danger just to prove a point.

But that kind of experience did toughen me up. When I was coaching in New Jersey, I coached Alonzo Mourning, one of the toughest guys in the league. That guy was a fighter on and off the court as he battled a kidney disease that nearly took his life.

The man loved basketball and was a competitor, but during one practice the Nets medical staff told me that due to his condition Alonzo wouldn't be able to play. I told him he'd have to sit, and he was not happy about it. He got right up in my face and started yelling at me. He's a big dude and all muscle, and he was maybe an inch from my face when he was yelling and screaming about being able to play.

I got it. He was frustrated. He's a competitor and he wanted to compete. But this was a matter of life or death, so I had no choice. When he got in my face, though, I didn't budge. I just stood there, looked him in the eye, and took it.

On the inside I was scared as hell, but on the outside you'd have had no idea because I was looking as if it didn't bother me. In that situation, I think it helped to let Alonzo know how serious the team thought this illness was. But in general, holding your ground is important. If you spend your life being bothered by everyone who tries to push you around, you can't be successful. You have to believe in yourself and your decisions in order to win the battle, even if it means taking a little abuse from time to time.

CHARLIE: PUTTING YOUR JOB ON THE LINE

I had a similar experience dealing with authority at McKesson Co. when a new president came in and right away, I could tell that he was not going to be an ally of water. He didn't care. You could see he didn't care. The first time he came down to our offices, he wasn't really paying attention to what we were showing him. He was checking his e-mail the whole time and barely listening. In that situation you grin and bear it.

I had one experience with him that was a real eye-opener for me. McKesson was a bricks-and-mortar company that was not a marketing company at all. It was in a very low-margin business of pharmaceutical distribution. At that point McKesson Water was primarily a home and office water cooler delivery business. I felt it was critically important for McKesson Water to stay current in the retail business, because even if you only break even at retail, you benefit from the display in the supermarket. It helps your brand and gives it credibility, which enables you to charge more money on the home and office side.

We had been in gallon, half-gallon, and two-and-a-half-gallon bottles, and I decided that we needed to be in the half-liter clear plastic bottles. It was very expensive to run small bottle production lines, but that was the direction retail was going in, and of course, if you're a water drinker today, you know very well that that's where the industry is thriving.

But this new president didn't want to spend the money for us to go into that market, because we couldn't justify the spending with retail alone, as opposed to the benefit retail would have to home and office. I believed that it was going to help our marketing and our overall ability to be successful as a company. We were butting heads on it, because I felt it was really important. He didn't like the idea, but I was getting some traction with the other senior management within McKesson Co. The head of strategic planning absolutely loved the idea, but he couldn't convince the president. What management agreed to do was bring in a consulting group and have it review our plans.

The consultants came in, did a thorough evaluation, and, much to the surprise of the president, they felt that not only should we invest in the half-liter clear plastic bottles, but in fact we should be doing even more than I had recommended. The president took the report, stuck it in his desk, and never shared it with anybody.

The head of strategic planning, though, went to the CEO and got him on board. At that point I felt that I had no choice. When I was making presentations to the board of directors on what we needed to do, I presented my ideas for retail water. I got them approved, and the president of McKesson Co. was not a happy camper.

I took a risk to benefit the company, not necessarily to benefit my own career. I'm willing to accept that my ideas aren't always the best. But I think you have to have an organization around you that believes the best idea is going to win. I think that's critical.

I knew this was the right direction, and today the single-serve clear plastic water bottle is bigger than soft drinks. I knew that was where the industry was going, and if we were going to be a bottled water company that was really a force to be reckoned with, then we had to be in that segment.

We had a 20 percent share of the bulk water business. Our brand was a big brand, and I knew we'd get placements in the store. We had good relationships with the buyers at the supermarkets. It was only a question of using the capital for that versus using it for something else. We ended up selling a lot of half-liter case goods off the route trucks as well.

It was the right decision, and even if I lost my job fighting for it, I was going to go down swinging because, no matter what my position is within a company, I'm always looking for a win.

BYRON: PUSHING BUTTONS TO BRING OUT THE BEST

In many cases the hard-line approach can be used for motivational purposes. When I was coaching in New Orleans, David West was one of our young star players. The only problem was that people didn't want to call him a star at first, so I needed David to use that to fuel his fire a bit.

He didn't come into the league with big expectations. He was the eighteenth pick overall in the 2003 draft, but at Xavier he had been talked about as a "tweener"—not big enough to be a power forward and not quick enough to be a small forward. Instead of looking at that as a negative, I tried to use it to motivate him. I'd point to him in our locker room and say, "People said you couldn't be an all-star, you're a tweener, you're not supposed to be good." That doubt pushed him to be his best. He always felt he had something to prove.

Whenever I thought he was getting a little complacent I'd remind him that there were many people who doubted him. "Continue to prove them wrong" is a great motivation for a lot of guys, because almost all NBA players have egos and play with a chip on their shoulder.

That's what made David tick. Just call him a tweener enough times and he'll play at an all-star level. You have to pick your moments to take those jabs, but as a coach you know when. Those instincts will kick in.

Not only was he an all-star in 2008 and 2009, he helped change the game by being that power forward who could dominate the boards and also hit shots from nineteen to twenty feet away. His skill set made him tough to guard. But in those seasons, he was playing with an edge. He was scoring for us on the box, and he was scoring for us from the perimeter.

The team dynamic helps, of course. When you are winning, the guys who are the best players on the team that season are going to be rewarded. Once the Hornets management started getting rid of players, the team changed and the momentum was lost. West never made another all-star team after that, but he always played at an all-star caliber.

The key, I believe, was knowing what buttons to push and staying tough with him whenever necessary. He was a tough guy, so he needed the tough love. When it's the right kind of player, it works.

CHARLIE: PUTTING YOUR MONEY WHERE YOUR MOUTH IS

When I was dealing with Tyson at Freshpet, it wasn't my job on the line, but I felt it was my obligation to fight because I thought my idea was what was best for the company.

I knew from that first phone call that that wouldn't be the last conversation about management. Some time later Freshpet needed a bridge loan in order to keep funding the business until one of the banks gave us a line of credit. But we needed money right away or we couldn't buy products or raw material. In order to get this bridge loan we needed to get Tyson's approval, because we needed personal guarantees from the senior investors.

I was taking a leisurely stroll through Central Park with my wife, Peggy, when I got a call from the three key people representing Tyson's interests.

"Guys, I need your Tyson guarantee in order to get a bridge loan," I said confidently.

"We're not willing to give you anything unless you agree to have the business moved to Arkansas and have us run it," one rep replied.

This was their chance. The CEO wanted to take over the company, and he'd sat back and waited until we needed Tyson for something—anything—to make a power play and demand we change our operations. I wasn't going to back down and let him tell me how this company should be run, so I told these gentlemen how I felt with a simple and direct response: "No way in hell. I'll personally guarantee it all myself."

It was a $3 million guarantee, which is a lot of money. They were shocked, but they couldn't do anything about it. Their CEO and senior management had told them to back us into a corner financially, and they hadn't really seen this coming.

I was not going to let them take the company from us and run it out of their headquarters. I firmly believed we didn't have a problem with management, but rather were going through the typical growing pains of a start-up.

Peggy had known what my position was before the phone call. We discuss these business matters all the time, and she is and always has been my best sounding board for important issues. It's a lot of money, $3 million, but I think she was proud of me for standing up for what I believed in.

I was so aggravated on the phone that I was trembling with rage, and I think she was concerned about that, but she wasn't all that concerned about losing the money.

So I moved forward without Tyson and personally guaranteed the money. After a few weeks the banks stepped up and gave us the line of credit that they'd said they would. Then the guarantee was lifted.

I didn't even ask for anything from Freshpet for putting up the money, because if I had asked for something I would again have had to get Tyson's agreement. By doing it without asking for anything, I left Tyson no recourse.

Shortly thereafter, the private equity firm MidOcean bought out Tyson, and Tyson moved on from its role in Freshpet, apart from a small equity position. Now we don't even use it for refrigerated distribution anymore.

MidOcean has a lot of investments in consumer packaged goods businesses, so it understands the vagaries of the early growth period. It knew that early fluctuation was normal and that everything was in place for future success. Like me, it wanted to see the company succeed. Together we thought this was the first big step in making that happen.

X's and O's

- Even when those above you are rooting for failure, your drive to succeed should never waver.

- There are times that you have to stand up for what you believe in. Folding early when you know you are right will lead to a loss of credibility.

- Combat negativity by having a thick skin and showing the team that under no circumstances will you be broken.

- There's no common approach to motivating everyone. Find what works for each team member and use it consistently.

Chapter 16

Temperament

"People won't have time for you if you are always angry or complaining." —Stephen Hawking

A lot of emotions come with success, and a lot of emotions get in the way of success, but controlled anger is essential for relaying a message. If you're going to yell, you want to make sure your voice is heard.

BYRON: OLD YELLER

In 2014, when I got the job as the head coach of the Los Angeles Lakers—a dream job considering my history with the team and the lifetime I spent in the Los Angeles area—I had grown as a coach. After thirty years as a player and coach I had seen just about everything happen in this league.

I knew what I was getting into with the Lakers roster, but I was confident that given the time I could turn it around. A sense of calm came over me as I signed a contract for only two guaranteed years, because I take people at their word. When Jim Buss and Mitch

Kupchak looked me in the eye and said they understood the process, it was enough for me to know that I'd have at least a third year.

Or course I was wrong, and I regret putting my faith in them. When they pulled the rug out from under me I was upset because I had been lied to. I'll never trust a deal that's not in writing again. It was a lesson learned.

Regardless of how many years I thought I was going to have, when I started I knew I had to be a different kind of coach with this team. We had a future Hall of Famer in Kobe Bryant, who was nearing the end of his career, and we had a bunch of young guys who were not championship ready. I knew that would really frustrate Kobe, and that it could easily frustrate me, but I had to keep my cool.

If I'm the type of coach who is always yelling, sooner or later the players are going to tune me out—especially in this league. Rick Adelman always said that you get five to seven times where you can really yell and scream and go off in the locker room. Any more than that and it just starts falling on deaf ears. If you don't do it often, you get their attention when you do raise your voice.

Trust me, there were plenty of times in the two years with the Lakers that I wanted to go off, but I did my best to hold it together. That wasn't always the case.

In my first couple of years as a head coach in New Jersey I went a little overboard as far as being a taskmaster and being tough with players. A lot of it was a combination of emulating what I was used to in a coach and trying too hard to make a statement. When Riles would challenge us, it got the best out of me. He would just go at you, and that worked with me. That's what I thought worked with everyone. But also I think I was trying to prove that I was ready to be a head coach.

There was one time when we came into the locker room after a game and Richard Jefferson, who was a young player at the time, wasn't happy because he wasn't getting a lot of touches. First of all, he was a rookie, and with me you have to earn those touches. Second of all, we'd won the game. So his complaining set me off. I just lost it. I was yelling and screaming and cursing the kid out.

It wasn't a calculated move. I wasn't trying to make him a better leader. I just lost my mind. I let him have it for five straight minutes, which is a long time when you're cursing and yelling.

A couple of weeks later I realized I had been way out of line. I should have apologized, but that's not something men do often with other men, especially in basketball. We kind of just know the person is sorry and move on without saying it.

I just moved forward and made sure I never did that again. To this day Richard Jefferson and I have a great relationship, which is a true testament to his character, since he never held that incident against me. He's a great kid, a hard worker, and a true professional, who last season added a well-deserved NBA championship to his résumé.

By the time I was coaching the Lakers my locker room rants were more calculated. If I'm going to really go off on someone, it's well planned out. Since you can really yell only a few times a season, you have to use them wisely. If you can get away without yelling at all, that's even better.

CHARLIE: CALCULATED ANGER

You spend your entire career learning to fight your emotions, and anger is one of the hardest to conquer. Anger is necessary sometimes. Yelling can be a positive if it is for the most part calculated. Generally you will lead by saying the right things in the right tone, but every now and then you'll want to yell.

At Freshpet we brought in a new CEO after Tyson had left and MidOcean had come in as a primary investor. There was a shift in direction based on the new team—one that I thought would help guide us in the right direction. The partnership with Tyson had seemed like a good idea at first, but once we realized it wasn't working we needed a fresh start.

Kicking off the new beginning was an investor presentation in which the new CEO was introduced and given the floor to talk about the future of the company. To start the meeting, the Freshpet management went over what had happened in the prior year and laid out a budget for the following year.

In the previous year, as in all the years prior, we hadn't met the budget. We had been way off in the number of new stores we projected we would get, so that had affected the numbers. As the management team began talking about the future, one of the investors, who was constantly critical, jumped in.

"Let's stop right here," he said. "Don't even bother showing the numbers. You never hit your numbers, so you're not going to hit these numbers. Why are we even doing a forecast?"

This particular investor was a pretty arrogant guy. He always had a complaint and a negative attitude. At that time it wasn't going as we had hoped, but his lack of respect for the management team wasn't helping.

When he made that comment, I just blew my stack. I told him it was total BS. If we didn't show a forecast he'd be complaining that we didn't have a forecast. As I was arguing, in the back of my mind I was thinking about how we had just brought this new CEO in and I had to protect him. I didn't want the investor group to sit there and take potshots at somebody who was just starting. You want someone like that to be encouraged and to know the investors are supportive.

Afterward, on the one hand I thought that I had somewhat lost control of my emotions, but on the other hand it had been the only way to firmly get the message across that we needed to be protective of the management team.

The rest of the room was a bit stunned, and for the most part silent. They hadn't seen this side of me before. But I couldn't just sit there and let a disgruntled investor sidetrack the whole presentation and the direction in which the company was going. If I had let that go unchallenged, the new CEO would likely have been questioning my support as chairman of the board representing the investor group.

It was a must-yell situation and it worked, because afterward we still had the support of the investor group, which was the most important thing. Plus it helped motivate the new CEO to strive for greatness. Looking back I know it was not just the right thing to do, but the only thing I could do.

BYRON: LEAD BY EXAMPLE

Instead of yelling all the time, what you have to do for the young guys is lead by example. I love the game of basketball. Few guys today look at it as we did, as something that you just love to do and you want to be the very best you can at. I think that for some of the guys today in the NBA, the game gets in the way of other things that they want to do. Practice definitely gets in the way, but to me practice was a highlight. I loved going to practice, working hard with my teammates, and getting better at basketball. The game we had that night was like the finale. It was the reward for the hard work.

To get guys to think along the same lines I had to be the first one in the gym and show that all these years later I still loved practice. I got up early in the morning and went to work out. A lot of those guys were just coming in when I was doing my workouts, and they saw that. Sometimes I was already on the court running and shooting when they were just strolling in.

When they saw that, they respected it. They saw that I wasn't afraid to do the work that I wanted them to do. It also kept me in as close to game shape as possible, so even at age fifty-five I had the ability to show them firsthand how I wanted something done. It helped.

On a winning team you want multiple players who also lead by example. On the Lakers we pretty much had only Kobe. He was a gym rat like me. Even in his rookie year, if there was an 11:00 a.m. practice, he would be on the court shooting at 8:00 a.m. He wasn't even a starter at that time, but he wanted to work. He loved it.

It helped that he had some veteran guys around him that rookie year. Guys like Nick Van Exel, Eddie Jones, Jerome Kersey, and Elden Campbell also knew the value of practice. Kobe followed their lead, but knowing him, I'm sure he would have been that way regardless.

In his final years Kobe was the same way, but he was a lone wolf out there. He didn't see the guys follow his lead, and he was rightfully frustrated. I was right there with him.

It's not just about winning. There are selfish reasons for working hard too, if that's what you need to motivate you. A lot of players in the NBA have been very talented and have become all-stars, but never won anything really significant. When they look back, they say, "Man, if I had just worked a little bit harder and taken a little bit better care of my body."

When you work hard you buy yourself more time. Jason Collins, whom I had in New Jersey, went to Stanford and was very intelligent and a very good basketball player with an outstanding work ethic. I think it allowed him to play as many years as he played. His name probably doesn't jump out in your mind as a star player's, but he put in thirteen seasons in the NBA, and I think he did that because he hustled in practice and took care of his body.

You don't have to be a Kobe Bryant to lead by example. Sometimes a Jason Collins can do it. Sometimes it's on me as a coach to do it. But in the end, young guys learn how to win by watching others act like winners, not by being yelled at to work harder.

CHARLIE: SET THE BAR

At every company I've been with, I've wanted to set the standard. I want the people around me not only to work hard but also to match my level of honesty and dedication to the company's success.

From day one at Nestlé or McKesson, or even as chairman of the board at Freshpet and other companies, if I said I'd get back to someone the next day, I got back to them the next day. If I said I'd have an answer for them by 5:00 p.m., they would have an answer by 5:00 p.m. If there was a meeting at 2:00 p.m., I was there on time. It sounds simple, but sticking to those little guidelines sets a tone for performance around the office. If I do it, others will follow suit without even being asked.

It starts with that example from me, and then the trust grows among the team. At McKesson people jumped on board quicker than I'd expected. There was a great deal of turmoil in the beginning, but people saw my personality and my work ethic and they believed in what I was trying to do. In return they began doing their jobs with few to no questions asked.

When it was time for us to acquire other businesses, the team had trust in me and I had trust in them. I could go to them and say, "Here's what we're working on, don't go home and tell your friends or spouses or dogs," and I knew they would stay loyal and abide by that request.

There was also no job too insignificant for me to do if the company needed it done. I think that came from my time at Deer Park, which was a smaller company where I was needed to do the small jobs often. That's how a small company is successful, but continuing to have that mind-set is also how a CEO at a big company is successful. You don't want to micromanage, but at the same time you have to be willing to do anything.

I was always ready to go on the bottling line to wash bottles, head out on the routes, or answer customer service calls in the call center. When it came to customers, not only would I take their call, I'd also follow up with a letter.

My wife Peggy's first cousin, John, worked for the real estate subsidiary of a Los Angeles bank. In the office they had Sparkletts as their water supplier. Unbeknownst to him, his boss called Sparkletts with a problem and the call made its way up to me. In most cases when the call makes its way to me, I want to fix the problem, but I'm also trying to sell the customer on how great the company is. Odds are, if the call lands in my lap, the person on the other end is really just looking to vent.

So I handled the call and followed up with a letter to confirm that we'd spoken and thank him for calling us. He didn't know I was John's cousin-in-law, but he showed John the letter. John laughed and told him we were related. John then came back to me and said it had made a huge impression on both him and his boss that I had done that.

These kinds of things also influence the other managers and employees in the job, and often in the rest of the business world. They see how a CEO should act, they move to jobs with that idea in mind, and ultimately they become that type of leader themselves. Obviously I want the company to succeed, so that's why I do it, but I want the people to succeed as well—not just now but forever. It's that mentality that creates a winning organization, and establishing that mind-set among the group starts with me.

BYRON: REALITY CHECK

When people don't follow your lead, and you don't want to become one of those coaches who yell all the time, you have to calmly hold people accountable. It might force you to make unpopular decisions, but in the end it's what is best for the team.

With rookies it's tough, because despite scouting you never really know what you're going to get. The first season with the Lakers we had Jordan Clarkson. Jordan had a great work ethic, loved being in the gym, and prided himself on working on his game. When he got a chance to play late in the season, he took full advantage of it, and the following year he was a starter for most of the year.

Jordan had been a second-round pick who many experts thought could be a lottery pick when he first decided to come out of college. He had a few bad workouts and his father was going through some medical issues, which probably affected him mentally. So he fell to us in the second round and played with a chip on his shoulder. He quickly became someone I could count on.

The second year we drafted D'Angelo Russell with the second pick overall in the 2015 NBA draft. A lot of pressure can come from being drafted that high, and also a lot of cockiness.

D'Angelo can flat-out shoot the ball, and he has point guard vision. His biggest issue for me was his willingness to work. He felt a sense of entitlement coming in, and being a starter on the Lakers didn't help that. I knew that if he didn't change his work ethic, he was going to be an average player in this league. But I also knew he had the potential to be great.

You want guys who want to be great, but as a coach you can also push them toward greatness. I have a rule that if you have three years' experience in the league or less, you have to be on the floor thirty minutes before practice and thirty minutes after practice for individual workouts. If you're not doing it voluntarily, then I'm going to make you do it.

Even with that, D'Angelo wasn't living up to his potential in games. An inflated ego, a poor work ethic, and the pressure of living up to the high draft pick were not a winning combination. The only solution was pulling him from the starting lineup.

There were multiple reasons for that decision. For one, he needed to learn that playing time was a privilege and not a right. People who practice hard and play the game the right way get to start. Second, I thought it would get the media off his back and shift the blame to me a little bit.

Expectations were high, so people were calling him a bust. But he was young and this was a whole new system for him, so he needed time to develop. As a coach I tried to deflect attention a little bit. When he wasn't playing, the questions from the media went away. I could just get up there and remind everyone that he was nineteen years old and that this was a process. I knew I was going to get him back in there eventually, and that when I did, it might just be the vote of confidence he needed to get him going in the right direction.

But when I benched him he reacted like most nineteen-year-olds and ran up to his room and called his agent to complain. The second I got to my room I got a call from Mitch Kupchak asking what had happened, because he had already received a call from D'Angelo's agent.

"I took him out of the starting lineup," I said. "I just feel that he thinks this is how it's supposed to be, that he's entitled to start."

We weren't playing well anyway, so shaking things up seemed like a good idea, and Mitch agreed. I sat both D'Angelo and Julius Randle (who was also not playing up to his potential) for around twenty games. When they came back into the starting lineup, they were totally different players.

They'd obviously gotten the message that they had to get better to earn the starting position. To their credit, they both did. I'd started them in the first place because I wanted to see what type of heart and toughness and mind-set they had. I'd wanted to see how they'd react to different situations. It didn't work out the first time, but by the second time I liked what I saw.

CHARLIE: SHOW THE VEIN, CONTROL THE VAIN

Early on in my time at McKesson Water, I was not popular with some of the people who had been there a long time. There was a senior manager in the grocery division, not too popular around the office, who was one of the guys out to get me. He was responsible for retail water, an area he'd spent many years working in, so he felt at that point he had earned the right to do things his way.

We were doing a full business review and I was asking all the division leaders questions. I asked him about his portion of the business, and he not only wouldn't answer the questions accurately, but also delivered his inaccurate answers with a bit of an attitude. It got to a point where he started questioning my knowledge in the grocery area—claiming I was just some direct delivery guy.

The irony there is that my background was consumer packaged goods, so I'd come out of the same space that he had. I'd known it better than the home and office business coming into this job. But for some reason he was set on trying to prove that I wasn't fit for the job, and that was infuriating.

When I get angry, I have a tell. A vein on the top of my head pops out whenever I'm mad—even if I'm speaking in a calm voice. Some of the people in the room noticed it, so they knew what was going on. I was angry, but it wasn't time to yell. Instead I calmly and methodically asked this guy questions.

He wanted to rile me up, but I wouldn't let him. My line of questioning caught him in a bunch of stories that didn't make sense, and it bothered him that I was so in control. He was embarrassed in front of the group, which had not been my intent, but it's what happens when a person comes in overconfident and angry and ends up losing a battle with someone who can calmly participate in a debate of sorts.

I'm an analytical person. I'm constantly evaluating the conversation as it's happening. I think I'm able to control my temper because of that. With some rare exceptions, when you get angry you aren't in control the way you need to be, and I like to be in control. In this situation I needed to be in control, or else I might have lost the whole room.

This guy was trying to push my buttons. He wanted me to lose the room. Had I gone off on him the way I might have wanted to, he'd be able to rally the rest of the division leaders behind him. He'd point to my anger, say that I had no business being CEO, and convince others I wasn't going to turn the company around.

That would have been a huge misstep for me. Instead, by handling it the way I did, I actually gained ground with the others in the room. This particular guy wasn't very liked, but I was still new, so people didn't know how they felt about me yet. After that meeting a number of people walked out with more respect for me. I know that because years later they told me.

The grocery division went through a bunch of turmoil early on. This particular guy had no respect for the person he reported to and he was always trying desperately to get him out so he could take his job. This meeting happened before we completed the consolidation, so he wanted to muscle his way into that role. But he wasn't the right person for the job, and shortly after, he left the company.

X's and O's

- You can only yell so much before people stop listening.

- Lead by example and the real winners will follow; yell at them to be better and they'll walk away.

- There is never a task too insignificant for you to take on if it helps the team improve.

- When discussing a difference with one person, always remember that the whole room is watching.

Chapter 17

Expectations and Credibility

"High expectations are the key to everything."—*Sam Walton*

A leader has to overcome the doubt of an organization and never stop believing that success is the only option. When times are tough your credibility may get called into question, but building trust and building confidence go hand in hand.

BYRON: CHANGING HABITS

When it comes to the success of a young team like that Lakers team, a lot of it has to do with expectations. A high draft pick like D'Angelo Russell may be expected to play at a certain level according to fans and the media. He may have certain expectations for himself. And I may have a whole different set of expectations for him as a coach.

You can motivate players to perform at their best when you define these expectations. Being a top pick is hard. There are a lot of so-called "busts." The pressure to perform is great, and a lot of people are relying on you.

When I got the job in New Jersey, we had the first pick in the

2000 draft and we took Kenyon Martin, who had the potential to be an all-star because of his intensity, athleticism, and tenacity on the basketball court. But because he was a first pick, people expected him to be an all-star right away, which is an even tougher task when the work ethic isn't there.

Kenyon was one of those guys who don't like practice. He was a game guy. He did everything at the bare minimum in practice, but when the game came on, he was a gamer.

I had to be tough with Kenyon to get the most out of him. I'd come into a huddle in the middle of the floor, look him dead in the eye, and explain how things were going to be done. I let him know that I was the boss. It wasn't a democracy, it was a dictatorship; my word was law and this was how practice was going to run. He could either fall in line or get out.

The irony is that the speech wasn't even for Kenyon, necessarily. I can live with a guy like him going through the motions at practice, because I know I'm going to get 110 percent from him in the game every single night. That's the type of guy he was, and I didn't mind that. But in order to get the most out of the entire team, I needed the other guys to see that I wasn't going to accept that from Kenyon. A lot of guys thought they could follow his lead, but they were less talented and couldn't pull it off. Those speeches were for them.

I kept the fire burning in Kenyon through our two trips to the Finals, and he eventually was named an all-star in the 2003–04 season for the first and only time in his career. I don't know if you can necessarily mold players into all-stars. I think what you try to do is give them all the necessary ingredients and insight so they can use their talents to the best of their capabilities.

You need three things to be an all-star: talent, intelligence, and work ethic. The first two, while you can always improve, you are pretty much born with. When it comes to work ethic, though, it's the coach's job to push the player to that all-star-caliber level.

To get the best possible outcome for a rookie, you've got to be very supportive and very positive, but you also have to let him see some of the things that he's doing wrong. Charlie likes to show the positives first, because if you don't do that, you lose people. In our field, when we do film sessions we show all the negative things first, because when we go on the court, we want the players' last impressions to be of the positive things that worked.

Whereas in business you can do your best work at different times, in basketball there is a set block of forty-eight minutes where you need to perform, so we need confidence high when the players are going on the court. They need to feel better about some of the things they're doing and better about the way we're playing as a basketball team. I always wanted to end on a positive note, to show them what they'd done right and drive home the point that we just needed to be more consistent.

CHARLIE: CREATE THE EXPECTATION

When you're managing expectations you have to manage up, you have to manage at your level, and you have to manage down. You have to create the expectation. What was always important to me was making sure everyone bought into the broader vision and goal. I always had to come back to reminding everyone what we could be and what we wanted to be.

At Freshpet, in times of trouble we were constantly keeping emotions stable and letting investors know we were on the right path. Even when we needed more money, we explained the situation and ended every meeting on a positive note. We never transmitted a sense of panic to the investors, or to the management team, for that matter. We had goals and we would push to meet them.

In the case of McKesson Water we wanted to be the best-run and most profitable water company in the world. We were absolutely shooting for the stars.

With corporate I had to set the expectation for how long the turnaround would take and let them know that there would be an earnings decline in the beginning. But I reminded them that the sun would rise again and that if we wanted the company to grow then these changes were necessary. Organizationally, within the company I had to explain to the survivors why the reduction of the workforce had been needed. Then, of course, I had to make sure I always stayed focused on the goals and didn't let a tanking California economy or any other obstacle stand in the way of my expectations.

What I did to keep expectations on track was hold a lot of meetings, and in those meetings I'd explain in depth—almost to a fault—where we stood as a company, and what we were doing to meet expectations. When things were down, I explained how we'd get them up. When things were up, I'd explain what we needed to do in order to avoid going down. I gave constant reminders of my expectations, and I think it kept the team working efficiently and striving for greatness.

I don't think there is such a thing as oversharing when it comes to business, especially during periods of change. I like to talk, but I like to listen even more. Meeting, talking, and explaining help everyone stay on the same page. I'm not telling people what to do in these meetings, I'm explaining what I expect and they are explaining what they need to meet those goals. At McKesson the meetings were frequent, and each one drove home the point of how we were going to get there.

The tone of the message was also important. I had to carefully relay every point I was trying to make. At McKesson Water, Sparkletts was really a family. The tenure of the average employee was probably eight years with the route drivers and ten-plus years with the rest of the company—both of which were extremely long. So when we were cutting from 2,500 to 1,500 employees, there was a lot of survivor guilt. I tried to be extremely sensitive to the fact that so many of the remaining employees' friends were losing their jobs. The message was that we weren't trying to be greedy in terms of accelerating our profits; we were trying to survive as an organization and be able to grow in the future.

What you say, how you say it, and the consistency of the message are all important. If you're not consistent with the message, people are going to take away whatever aspects of it support the feelings they had going in. If they want to be negative, they'll pull the negativity out if you don't consistently drive home the point that the plan will work if the company stays the course.

The people who had lost their jobs still had an emotional tie to the company and, because of their long tenure with McKesson Water, they were still in the ear of many of their friends who remained. From the sidelines many were rooting for the change to fail, so it was important that those same employees hear my voice in their other ear, constantly reminding them why we wouldn't fail.

The negativity affected some people, but once they began to see how they were getting new tools to work with and a new software enterprise package with streamlined data for easier decision making, the momentum started to swing in my favor. The improvements at the company, along with the constant driving home of the message, were a wake-up call for people. They realized they actually could turn this thing around and that they could have a role in making success happen.

When you sell the message, deliver on promises, and motivate people to be the change agents, success happens. It took about four years to get out of the dark period, but we did it in large part by constantly saying we were going to do it, believing in our goals, and giving everyone the tools to meet expectations.

BYRON: SETTING THE BAR HIGH

As a competitor I always wanted to win. I knew this Lakers team was flawed, but I still expected to go out there and compete every single night. Even in Cleveland after LeBron left, I had high expectations for the team.

The Decision—as it is now famously called—was in July, so we had three months to settle in and think about how we were going to approach the season. The players had the time to think about it, mull it over, and then get ready for a new era.

I didn't have any ties with LeBron, so it was easy for me to move on, but I understood the disappointment. They were used to winning, and instead of going out there and fighting, it is often easier to just switch off and accept losing.

It was my job to come in and get rid of that attitude right away. This was a new day, a new atmosphere, and a whole new team. That's what I told the guys on the first day of practice. I said, "We expect you guys who have been here to step up, be leaders, play whatever role necessary, and continue to be winners."

Sometimes guys step up and accept the challenge, and sometimes it's on the coach to find the leaders. In that case it was on me. The veterans on the team had spent so long playing behind LeBron that they didn't immediately remember how to play without him.

LeBron had made all those guys better on the court, and I was asking them to do something that they hadn't had to do for a few years—step up their game and be the best versions of themselves, and, most importantly, win games.

"Guys," I said on day one, "I want to go out there and win. That's the bottom line. We still want to be a playoff basketball team."

There was a mix of looks on their faces. You could tell some of them were up for the challenge and others were already planning early summer vacations.

"A lot of guys are going to have to step it up. But I have a lot of confidence in everybody here that we can get it done."

I believed in them. They needed to know that. It's important to not just imply it but also say it as the team leader. *I have confidence in you* are probably the most important five words you can say as a coach.

It was the same way with this Lakers team. Kobe wanted to win, but at his age he couldn't do it on his own. Players needed to step up in a way that they never had in order to win. I had confidence in them, and I told them that as often as I could.

The key is, you have to mean it. Players can tell when you're blowing smoke up their butts. I believed it because I believed in me. If we did all the things we had to do in training camp and the preseason to get ready for the regular season, then we had a chance to be successful.

Work hard and play together as a basketball team and anything is possible. In Cleveland I never mentioned LeBron once he left. He was already gone, so why even mention him? I was all about looking toward the future. It didn't matter what he'd done the year before. It didn't matter what anyone had done.

Despite the lack of success in Cleveland, I took that same mentality to Los Angeles. What choice did I have? I wasn't talking championship, but I thought making the playoffs was a legitimate goal. If you don't strive for greatness, then there's really no reason to get out of bed in the morning. In order to win you have to expect to win and then go out and make it happen.

CHARLIE: MINI GOALS TOWARD LOFTY DREAMS

I always want to win and I truly always believe I will. That's the only way to be successful. I believe in myself, and I believe in the team around me once I've put that team together.

It's the way I've been my whole life. When I decided to run the New York City Marathon, I set mini goals that led to my bigger goal, and ultimately I was able to complete the marathon.

I've done that in a number of areas with work as well. If I wanted to get something done by a specific date, I always laid out the steps I had to follow along the way in order to make it happen.

So it's not just telling yourself or your team that you're going to win, it's about thinking out the steps to actually get to the victory parade. For example, let's say you want to become a better communicator. If you're a manager at any level, you'll need to be able to talk to people the right way in order to motivate them to put forth their best effort.

To improve your overall communication skills, you might first tell yourself that you are going to improve your active listening skills. Every time you talk to somebody, you're going to ask them three different questions before you get off the subject they started.

By doing that you're doing two things: telling them you really care about what they're saying and getting them to open up a little bit so you can learn more about them.

In exchange for that, you share something with that person that you wouldn't normally share. Do that twice a day and you'd be amazed at how quickly it starts to become more natural. Listening and speaking go hand in hand. Conversations are a two-person job, and once you learn to listen, your communication skills will drastically improve.

That works on an individual level and on a team level. One of the things I truly believe is that as a team you're only as strong as your weakest player. If one person isn't carrying their weight or doing what they need to be doing, it brings everybody down. You want a group around you that isn't afraid to strongly voice its opinions, and I think I did a very good job of enabling everyone to have a voice. So there was never a meeting where it was my decision. I'd hear everyone out and we'd come to an agreement, and almost every time it was a group decision.

When you're on a board and not the operator, the control isn't totally in your hands, but your expectations are high. You can't set mini goals for yourself, but you can push the CEO to stay on track with the goals the board lays out.

Each investment opportunity is different, but that doesn't change your dedication to success. Whether you're playing off a trend that is starting and you're in it for the long haul, as with Freshpet, or there is an opportunity to make changes and flip a company for a quick profit, as with Day Runner, the mind-set needs to be the same.

We turned Day Runner around in two years and sold it because that category was disappearing in the face of handheld computers. The category was a trend that was dying, not a trend that was taking off. Was I in love with that company the way I am with Freshpet? No. Did I want to win just as badly? Absolutely.

I invested my own money and other people's money, and if I commit to something, I'm going to give 110 percent of my effort to execute what I've committed to. I'm not falling in love with it, but I'm passionately following up on my commitments.

You might not marry your high school sweetheart, but while you are dating you have to believe you have a future together. Successful people can't turn it on and turn it off. When you do something, you're going to try to do it the best you can. When the mission seems impossible, you just want to push even harder.

BYRON: EARNING CREDIBILITY

When I go into practice and tell a team that I expect to win, there are some who probably roll their eyes. Some jump on board, but others either don't believe or don't respect me enough to believe.

For the most part, I get that credibility and that respect pretty much when I walk in the door, because they already know who I am. They know that I won championships. It resonates with the players right away. I don't have to come in and pound my chest or try to play like I'm some big tough guy. I just come in and be myself.

I talk to them about what we have to do as a basketball team, not what we did back in the day, mainly because we don't have the players to do what we did back in the day. If you are coaching and trying to get a guy to try to play like Magic Johnson, that's a lot of pressure and expectations he'll never live up to.

Plenty of them have watched the old games on ESPN Classic or know a little about the history of the league, but the older I get, the further I'm removed from my playing days, so some of the respect may start to dwindle.

In some cases I've probably walked in thinking I had credibility with the guys when I didn't. It's a very what-have-you-done-for-me-lately league, and one of my flaws is that I sometimes forget that.

With a new season, you often have to go out and earn that credibility all over again—especially if you have no NBA playing experience. A lot of players will look at a coach who never played and not give him the respect he deserves right away. Coaches can earn that respect quickly, and a coach like me can lose respect just as fast if the players feel he doesn't know what he's doing or that they can just run right over him.

My son Thomas was an assistant coach/player development coach with me with the Lakers. As the coach's son who also had never played in the NBA, he had to work twice as hard to gain respect, but when you are good at what you do it happens quickly.

When I first got the job with the Lakers, Kobe called and we talked about the offense because he wanted to know the specific places where he would be touching the ball on the floor so he could go and work on those spots. After we got done discussing strategy, he told me he wanted Thomas to go to Germany with him to work out.

When Thomas decided to go over there with him, I sat down with him and explained what we were going to run for Kobe and where he needed to be on certain plays to get the ball. Then I shipped him off to Germany. They worked their butts off to come into that first season with a good understanding of the system.

Thomas came back and was amazed at Kobe's work ethic and

everything he did to prepare. Kobe could coast. It didn't matter as far as his legacy goes. Plus he knew he wasn't going to win a championship that season. But Kobe has only one gear, and it's giving 100 percent all the time. I don't think that leaves you, no matter what stage of your career you're in. Kobe, even going into his nineteenth year, wanted to know all the little details about where he would be on the court so he could be ready for training camp. He always wants to win, no matter what situation he's in.

The workout was huge for Thomas's credibility. Jordan Clarkson knew he'd worked out with Kobe, so when we were in training camp he gravitated toward Thomas. The following year D'Angelo Russell did the same.

When you spend the summer working with Kobe, other guys get curious and want to see what you've got. They respected Thomas, and when they worked together a bond developed. Then Thomas became a coach with credibility, someone everyone wanted to work with.

It happens differently for every coach. On my staff in Los Angeles there was Paul Pressey, who'd played in the league and had also been an assistant coach for more than twenty years, so guys looked up to him. Mark Madsen may not have had the best dance moves, but everyone remembers that victory parade, so in my mind that ring gives him instant credibility.

In Thomas's case, I started him in New Orleans in the video room and let him work his way up. I wanted to make sure I gave him every opportunity to be a coach and tried to put him in the right position to do that, but I also wanted him to earn it.

He moved up to player development coach, then to assistant coach for the Development League team and up the ranks until he was qualified to be an assistant coach. I'd always had dreams of his being on the bench with me, but I'm extremely proud of him because he did it the right way. I think that's what Kobe saw in him too.

CHARLIE: BUILDING TRUST TO MEET EXPECTATIONS

It doesn't matter if you are a young manager just starting out or a gray-haired veteran in your industry, credibility always comes into play. No matter whose expectations you are managing, you need the people on the receiving end of the message to trust you.

For the bulk of the time that I've been chairman of the board at Freshpet, it has been a private company. The shareholders were the investor group, and managing their expectations was a difficult challenge, because I wanted to keep them totally in the loop, but also keep them encouraged that the company was going in the right direction. At that time, since we were not meeting expectations, we asked the investor group to put more money into the business and at the same time guarantee bank loans. It made managing expectations all the more difficult.

I tried to give a consistent message. We were never going backward and losing stores that we had, we just weren't growing nearly as fast as we'd thought we would be. Selling to the retail trade was much harder than we had originally thought. I'd focus on the positives and reiterate the long-term growth potential of our business to show that we were on the right track. Since I was being sincere with my message and because of my past successes as a CEO and investor, people believed me. I had the credibility needed to keep spirits high during tough times.

Originally we'd thought Freshpet would grow a lot faster and a strategic buyer would come along and buy the company. As we started growing we saw there was a great public market for a high-growth, small-capital company and recognized we could get a higher price by going public than we could by selling to a strategic buyer.

McKesson was a publicly traded company, but the water division was a small division within that company, so I had only a little taste of what it was like to be a CEO in a publicly traded company. (I had exposure to analysts, especially when our division didn't hit its goals and the stock of our company was severely affected.) Glacier Vending was public, but it was so thinly traded that a small number of people had voting control of the company. Neither of my roles at those companies compared to my new role as chairman of the board of a truly publicly traded company. Freshpet has a lot of investors and a lot of shares trading, and it was my first time being a chairman of the board at that level.

Even at my age, credibility comes into play in a situation like this. My role as chairman of a public company is to make sure that we have the right people in the right roles, and I certainly have a loud voice in discussions about whether the guidance we're giving to financial analysts is good guidance or not. Since I had the prior experience with Freshpet and a lifetime of successfully putting the right people in the right roles, I was still the right person to carry out the expectations of this company.

There's definitely a difference between being chairman of the board of a private company versus a public company. I'm no longer directly dealing with the investor group I was representing. Now the investor group is the public. I have no direct access and I'm not directly influencing the public investors. It's going through the CEO and CFO, who are dealing with analysts sending out their quarterly guidance to investors, and explaining where they think the company is headed.

The board is trying to protect all the public investors, so we're looking at what's in the best interests of the company over the long term. Our governance is around making sure that we have the right people in the right places, and we're managing how money is being allocated and making sure we are doing everything possible to maximize returns for public investors.

We want to make sure that we are being totally honest and not overpromising. We want to give encouragement to investors so the world agrees with us that this is a great company. But we also have to manage short-term expectations against long-term direction.

As a leader of the board, every day you have to constantly talk about the best business decisions to grow the business, and how the CEO can best explain what we're doing to the analysts and our shareholders. I'm not the voice of the company, but I'm the voice in the ear of the voice. If I relay my expectations confidently and everyone listening trusts me, the CEO will pass on the message in the same way.

X's and O's

- Define expectations for people and allow them to live up to their potential.

- You have to manage up and manage down and create realistic expectation at all levels of the organization.

- Credibility is partially earned by what you've done in the past, but it is also earned by what you are doing today.

- Honesty of expectations and consistency of the message delivered will lead to credibility even in the toughest of times.

Chapter 18

Heads and Hearts

"We cannot negotiate with those who say, 'What's mine is mine and what's yours is negotiable.'" —*John F. Kennedy*

In any negotiation, you have to understand the wants and needs of the person on the other side. To make a deal, everyone needs to feel they are walking away a winner.

BYRON: SELLING SUCCESS

Once you have the respect of the players, you have to use that respect to your advantage and speak to the players in a way that gets them excited about the opportunity of winning. Everyone wants to win, and that should be the focus from day one—actually from before day one.

In LA we didn't do a good-enough job of selling that winning mentality, especially when it came to trying to bring in free agents. In an attempt to improve our roster, management tried to coax LaMarcus Aldridge into putting on the purple and gold. He was a star player and a difference maker and would have helped push the team to the next level.

I wasn't in on the meetings prior to his coming in, so I don't know what was discussed or what plan was formulated, but in the big first meeting everything but basketball was discussed.

Lakers COO Tim Harris was running the meeting with Jim Buss, and they talked about the movie business, other businesses at Time Warner, and other avenues that one could pursue in business in Los Angeles. "Whatever you're interested in we have it here in LA" was sort of the running theme in that meeting. There were probably ten or fifteen people in the room, and only Mitch Kupchak, James Worthy, and I were there to talk about basketball.

Mitch and I both sat quietly. I was sitting there the whole time wondering when we were going to hit the topic that we really needed to hit, but I rolled with the punches and kept my mouth shut. When we finally did have the opportunity to start talking about basketball, we'd already been sitting there probably an hour and a half.

That's not how it should be done. When I was in New Jersey, management brought Aaron Williams to the office and to dinner and we talked about basketball. We told him how we thought he would fit in, told him who else we were trying to get, and even talked about playing time. I told him right there that he'd have to earn his playing time, and he appreciated it. Good players want to work for their success.

He wanted to win, and when we told him we had four picks in the following year's draft, he knew we had a chance to be pretty good. That's how it's supposed to go. He wanted us and we wanted him.

In New Jersey you can live in Manhattan and have all the outside opportunities that you'd have in LA, but we didn't talk about that once. That's not what he wanted. That's not what we wanted either. What good is it going to do me if a guy on my team moves to New

York because he wants to star on Broadway or moves to LA to put out a rap album? That's not what I want out of a leader on my team, so why would I want to sell a player on those opportunities?

In the end, I think the player has to be true to what he wants, but we have to go in having a good feeling about what he wants too. If management can get some insight from his agent, his brother or sister, his mother or father or a close friend, that helps, but somehow, some way the homework has to be done.

LaMarcus was stoic through it all when we sat with him in LA. He wasn't reacting one way or another. He listened and nodded, but the whole time he probably couldn't believe what he was hearing. Obviously, afterward we found out he wasn't interested in any of that and he just wanted to hear about how we were going to help him win. That's the kind of player you want on your team, yet ironically, it was the last thing the team wanted to focus on.

Luckily for us, he gave us a second chance to come in and talk about winning basketball games. But by then it was too late. He decided to sign with the Spurs, a team in a city where he will be very unlikely to launch his movie or music career.

CHARLIE: TEAM BUILDING THE RIGHT WAY

Luring talent to join your team is a skill that cannot be handled lightly if you're trying to assemble the best possible players. You have to get into the heads and hearts of the people and understand exactly what they need.

At Day Runner I convinced two very important people to come to work there: the CEO and the head of marketing. Both of them were in good jobs before they came to us, so I carefully showed them how they could make a lot of money in a short time. I outlined the tasks that they needed to get done, and told them that if they got them done, we'd all be very wealthy.

One had been a corporate officer in the drug division at McKesson, and the other my head of marketing at McKesson Water. The class of trade that we were selling to was one both of them had a lot of experience in. Walmart, the largest customer of McKesson Corp., was also the largest customer of Day Runner.

There was no beating around the bush in these negotiations. I wanted them and I laid out the benefits of their joining the team.

People want to be on a winning team. If I'm running a division and that division never hits the budget and never makes bonuses, and one year after the next we're far behind where we ought to be, it's demoralizing. And at some point you say, "I want to go someplace where I'm having fun and we're winning." At the end of the day, if the company is winning in the marketplace, growing share and making more money year after year, then the people get paid appropriately and have opportunities for nice bonuses. No one leaves a job when that's the case. Even if they get an offer for a little bit more money, they likely won't leave.

With these two people, I saw a window and I took it. In one case it was just a matter of explaining the business opportunity, since she had worked with me in the past. In the other case the person needed to feel wanted, so I had to play to that. He had a house in Florida and was living in Chicago, and I just said, "Look, if you need to go back and forth, you go back and forth. We need you to do this. You are the perfect person to get it off the ground." It was true, but he also needed to hear it.

Both came to Day Runner, and we were all in it together until we sold the business. The one guy, Mark Majeske, had his wife and family stay in Chicago while he rented an apartment near the office in

Fullerton. He would spend three or four days a week there and then head back home. When he was traveling for the company, I didn't care where he departed from. What I cared about was that he and his people fixed the product mix, fixed the supply chain on manufacturing and in delivery and distribution, and got the right salespeople in place.

This was a short-term move, and I made that very clear. Everyone knew we wanted to be out in three years, so I had to be flexible and make sure the members of the team were able to perform. When people come into a company, some of them are already thinking about what they need to do to get promoted to the next job instead of how to do their current job to the very best of their ability. But if you perform and meet or exceed expectations, people will notice and it will ultimately be rewarded.

At Day Runner, both of these leaders had the right incentives in place, and they made a lot of money. I got what I wanted, but so did they.

BYRON: HEAD GAMES

Even when you're focused on winning, the business side of basketball can easily get in the way of playing winning basketball. Guys can get traded at any time, they have contracts and finances to worry about, and all of it can get in their heads.

It was simpler back when I was a player. When my rookie contract was up after my fourth year, Jerry West came to me and said, "You're leading us in scoring. You're an integral part of this team. Think about how much you want and how many years you want on your contract."

I was about to answer him right away, but he stopped me.

"No," he said. "Just think about it."

Shortly after, my ex-wife and I took a trip to Israel to see the birthplace of Christ. I'm a Christian and my father's an ordained minister, so that was a trip I'd wanted to take for a long time. We went into all the little temples, saw exactly where he was born, and walked down a pathway where he walked.

It made my wife and me feel closer to Christ. Having faith in something that you can't see and being able to go to his gravesite—it was remarkable to us. Just thinking about it gives me chills, and it's been thirty years since that trip.

I never took religion for granted because I've always been a believer, but being able to go to the site and walk some of the paths that our heavenly Father walked was something I had never imagined as a child. It changed my life to understand that prayers can be answered.

While we were in Jerusalem, everybody there was writing down their goals and sticking them in the Wailing Wall. I was fresh off that conversation with Jerry West, so I wrote on a piece of paper that I wanted a four-year deal at $1.1 million a year and stuck it in the wall.

As I was folding it up and sticking it in, I closed my eyes and I said a prayer: "Heavenly Father, these are the things I want to accomplish in the next four or five years. I come to you and I ask these things in your name."

I ended up getting that four-year deal for $1.1 million a year. It was stress-free compared to what guys go through today. A little prayer goes a long way, but these days some of these guys need a miracle.

Either way, I'm a true believer in writing goals down. You probably want to put them somewhere where you can look at them every now and then and not in a wall, but that was a special note for a special moment.

Even today I like writing out five-year plans. I just put them in a place where I know I can get to them every so often to remind myself that those are things I want to accomplish, so I don't get sideways.

When you have a plan, you can better focus on the present goals like winning basketball games. If your head is bogged down by contracts or other business ventures, winning starts to slide down on your list of goals. In a perfect world it all happens as easily as it did for me, but when it doesn't, a player has to do his best to stay focused and a coach has to do his best to keep the player on track.

CHARLIE: THE BOND OF THE DEAL

When I'm negotiating, I never want to get what I want at another person's expense. I want both parties to walk away happy, and I need the other party to trust me that we will. You get more when the person on the other end of the deal isn't worried that you are trying to swindle them in any way.

One time I was in a market in Lagos, Nigeria—a huge market that was open every Sunday—where a lot of artisans brought their wares. It was a square mile of stalls that were up and gone in a day. Within the culture of Nigeria are four or five major tribes, and one of them is the Hausa. The Hausa are nomadic and travel from market to market selling their goods.

I went to one stall and this particular merchant had a beautiful bronze statue. It was an absolutely gorgeous two-foot statue of a woman carrying a baby in a basket on her back. It was spectacular and I wanted it.

The dealer wanted 2,500 naira (around $4,000 American in 1975), which was far more money than I wanted to pay for it. I had no idea what it was worth, but I said I'd pay 200. We spent hours bickering and I got up to maybe 800 and he dropped from 2,500 to maybe 1,600, but there was still a big spread, and I said, "Sorry, I'm not going one naira higher." He said he wouldn't go one naira lower, and we were done. When you don't get what you need, you can't be afraid to walk away.

I went back the next Sunday, and the guy was there. He had that same beautiful bronze statue, and I still really wanted it.

"Make me an offer," he said.

"Well, what do you think it's worth?"

"Two thousand five hundred naira."

"I think it's worth two hundred."

We negotiated again for several hours, and in the course of the negotiation we got to know each other, but we still ended without a deal.

Four Sundays in a row I went back, and four Sundays in a row I found him and we had the same experience. Neither of us was willing to budge. On the fifth Sunday, I didn't even go to his stall. He came and he found me (which was amazing to begin with given the size of the open market) and said, "I'm going to make you an offer, but if you ever tell anybody I've given you this deal, I'm going to come back and I'm going to kill you."

He needed money and was leaving, so he offered the statue to me for 1,000 naira. "You have a deal," I said, but the statue he gave me was not the same one that I liked. It didn't have the baby in the basket. "I know why you did that," I said. "Because it's not the same one."

"I have six of them and I just bring one each week," he said. "I just didn't bring the right one. Take it, don't give me any money, but come back next Sunday, and I will have the other five, and you can pick whichever one you want and then you can pay me."

He was out of his mind. Lagos then had a population of three million people. He didn't know me from a hole in the wall. How did he know I was going to come back?

"I've been negotiating with you for four Sundays in a row," he said. "I think I know you, and if we shake hands, I know you're going to come back."

Sure enough, I took it and came back the next Sunday, when he had the other five statues, including the one I liked, and we did the deal.

Two really important lessons can be learned from this. One is that you need a lot of time to negotiate. If you are in a hurry—if you have to have something—you will never get the best deal in a negotiation. The second lesson, which has stayed with me, is that in order to get what you really want, you need to have somebody like you and want to work with you. I wasn't always great at talking to people. That developed over time. But when I talk to anyone, in a negotiation or otherwise, I mean what I say and I genuinely care about the other person's happiness. People pick up on that, and overall it helps deals get done.

BYRON: WINNING FOR YOU

Today's NBA is far different from the one I played in. The kind of relationship I had with Jerry West is rare today, if not nonexistent. Everything seemed easier when it came to contracts and loyalty and overall happiness in relationships with the executives in the organization.

Maybe I just got lucky, but it seems today that even though the players make a lot more money, you see a lot more guys letting the money get in their heads while they are playing. As a coach I try to be honest with them. I tell them, "Get as much money as you can.

It is a business and you are in it to make money, but you also want to leave a legacy in this business."

If you ask most guys on the teams I coach how many rings I won, they'll know the answer is three. But if you ask them how many points I scored in my career, they'll have no idea. The point is, when you win in this league nobody ever forgets that, but all the stats (unless you hold the record) get forgotten. The legacy you leave is based on winning, so when players are out there only thinking about their individual success, they are focused on the wrong thing—not just for the team but for their own legacy.

That's what I try to tell the guys when they are in a contract year and letting thoughts about their future affect the way they are playing. You can't go out there and play for next year while the team is focused on winning now. But basketball is a business, and guys today are building a brand and collecting checks in all sorts of business ventures, so it's tempting to lose focus.

In my second year coaching the Lakers, Jordan Clarkson's contract was up at the end of the season. There was a buzz in the media that he had the potential to go from six figures to more than $6 million a year. In a perfect world he would block all of that out, but obviously it was on his mind.

His agent was telling him he had to have a great year. His friends and family were probably counting on him. It's stressful for a young guy, and obviously the instinct is to go out there and shoot more.

But more shots led to bad shots, and he wasn't hitting open guys with passes, and it started to hurt the team and his own numbers. Midway through the season, I pulled him aside during practice.

"Last year you averaged fifteen points, just like you're averaging this year," I said. "But your shooting percentage is down and your assists are cut in half. I know your contract is up, but if you keep going on this path you're going to devalue yourself. Everybody knows your contract is up, and most people can tell what you're doing out there. It's not working because that's not who you are. Just go out and play, be unselfish, and be the Jordan Clarkson who deserves that contract."

Talking to him about his actions that were affecting his own future was the way to get into his head. Had I talked about his hurting the team it might have gone in one ear and out the other because he was so distracted by the contract that he couldn't even think about the team.

Instead I spoke to his specific concerns, and it made a difference. I got what he was doing and I understood it, but if he really wanted to get paid he couldn't be a selfish player. GMs and coaches see that and don't want to add that to their roster. Just as with legacy, all that really matters is a guy's ability to win.

CHARLIE: WHAT'S IN IT FOR ME?

There is no better feeling than the feeling of winning. Whether it's joining a team and being part of the team's success or negotiating a deal and getting what you want, winning is the ultimate high. It's perfectly normal to chase that high in any business deal you do.

It's OK to make it about you. Even when you are making sure the other person walks away happy too, that's ultimately a negotiating tactic that gets you what you want. It's not selfish; it's good business.

In any negotiation, I need to know going in exactly what I need, why I need it, and what the other person is going to need. If I can't balance those, I'm not going to be successful with the negotiation.

At Deer Park we were using wooden crates with glass bottles, and one day the crate manufacturer came in and said he needed to get a price increase.

When you are in the product business you really have to understand the category you're dealing with and know the positioning of every product you're competing with in that category. You have to know how you're differentiating your product from the competition's. That difference can be in price, size, service, ingredients—there are all kinds of metrics that can differentiate you.

But the product is, of course, the most important thing, and everything is centered on price value. At Deer Park and Sparkletts, we were more expensive than most of the competition. We had to justify that by giving better service and having impeccable product quality. Otherwise why would you pay more for it?

With wooden crates it was the same thing. Other companies were offering better prices for metal racks and plastic crates that were better quality. The wooden crate supplier provided good service but nothing exceptional that would lure me into paying more for his product, so I didn't really see the point in sticking around if he wanted to raise the prices.

He claimed that his costs were going up. He assumed I didn't want to put in the effort to find a new company or even spend any part of my day negotiating, so he thought a small price increase would be an easy win for him. It wasn't.

In a very quick negotiation I explained to him how easy and likely more cost effective it would be for me to find another supplier. After a couple of minutes he knew he didn't have a leg to stand on.

After we were done negotiating he ended up decreasing the price of the wooden crates. In any negotiation, you have to have a really good reason to ask for anything, you have to be able to justify it, and you have to be willing to accept the consequences if you're not successful. A good negotiator knows what the limit is and is willing to turn around and walk away if they can't get whatever it is they are trying to get.

This guy didn't really think things through, and in this case I had to look out for what I needed for the company and myself as CEO. Did he want to make more money? Sure. Did he need to make more money? Maybe. But I couldn't be concerned with his needs when he wasn't concerned with mine.

Sometimes after a good negotiation I've been invited to a person's house for lunch or dinner. Sometimes people have just given me things because they were so happy with what they were getting. Those things have happened to me here in the United States and all over the world. If you can get somebody to genuinely like and respect you, and they believe you really care about them, they'll work so much harder and so much better for the good of the company than they would if they didn't feel that way. This crate guy was just trying to make a quick buck, and instead of taking me for lunch he was taking me for a ride. Needless to say, his plan (or lack thereof) backfired immensely.

X's and O's

- Write down your goals and remind yourself of them every day.

- Genuinely care about the other person's happiness and you'll likely get what you want in return.

- Be a daily planner and a big-picture thinker at the same time.

- Know exactly what you want and at what cost before entering a negotiation.

Chapter 19

Farewells

"Parting is such sweet sorrow, / That I shall say good-night till it be morrow." —*William Shakespeare,* Romeo and Juliet

In a perfect world you'll always go out on top, but regardless of how it ends, the wins are what are remembered. Before you choose your next adventure, take time to reevaluate your goals and your definition of success.

BYRON: NEVER CHANGE

Relationships change over the course of a lifetime. As I moved from player to assistant coach to head coach I always wanted to make sure I stuck to my core values and treated people with the same respect regardless of my position with the team. If I do that, and the other person can do that as well, relationships can grow into even deeper, more meaningful bonds.

Gary Vitti, for example, was still the head trainer with the Lakers when I returned to coach. This time around we were much older and in different places in our lives—married, then divorced, and now in new relationships. He'd call me the big kahuna or head honcho, because I was the coach now. But the relationship between us was still the same.

There's nothing that I wouldn't do for Vitti. We go to dinner with James Worthy and the wives and girlfriends and tell stories about back in the day when he was a young Gary Vitti and James and I looked exactly the same as we do today. The fact that all these years later we can still get together and talk like that is proof that relationships matter.

On the court it was the same way. He's gotten much more blunt in his old age, but the players respect it, because they know he's seen and done it all in his career. In his first four years with the Lakers he won three championships, so thirty years later he'd be the first to tell the current team they ain't nothing compared to the players we had back in the day. He'd say it casually and I would crack up laughing because that's Gary Vitti.

That's just the way he is; he's going to tell you like it is. He's not going to pull any punches—and that's even with me. He's just as straight up with me as he always has been, and that's what I love about him.

That's part of what's special about being a Laker. The trainer has eight championships in his thirty years. Magic and Worthy are in the building all the time. You don't get that anywhere else. Often I told guys over the course of the most recent two years that this uniform is like no other uniform that you ever put on. The team is like no other team that you'll ever be a part of. The legends and Hall of Famers who walk through these halls still got mad love for this organization. They know what it's all about, so it takes a different type of person with a different level of pride to put on the Lakers uniform and walk the halls with them.

Once you put it on, as Magic Johnson says, there are no excuses. I don't want to hear that you're sick or your knee hurts. I don't want to hear that garbage. If you put the uniform on, you better be ready to play. Period.

That's how I felt. That's how Gary Vitti felt. That's how everyone who bleeds purple and gold feels. It took some time, but that's how the guys on the team started to feel as well.

Larry Nance Jr. went to Vitti a few times for advice. Lou Williams would go to him. They knew, as I did as a player, that the winning mentality in the organization flowed through Gary Vitti, and whether he was solving a life problem or teaching you how to properly lift weights, he was making you a better winner.

Of course, he stuck by his core values too, which is why he'd never tell me what he and the players talked about.

"That's between me and them," he'd tell me when I'd try to squeeze it out of him. "Big kahuna, I got to keep this to myself, because I told them it was between me and them."

That's the code and I respect that. The fact that he never wavers in his beliefs is what makes him a winner. In fact, it's what made all of us winners. For us to win championships the training staff had to be doing its job, the medical staff doing its job. It's not just the coaches and players on the floor. It's everyone. That's why everyone gets a ring.

CHARLIE: FINISH LINES

Companies are defined by the people who work for them. From top to bottom, it's the team that makes it a success. At Deer Park I had to manage up to Nestlé. I had to manage out to the unions. I had to manage and get the best pricing and service quality from the copackers who were bottling the water. My job was really to get the resources I needed from Nestlé, keep it apprised of the issues I had so it didn't have any angst about what I was doing, and find the resources and the talent to let that company grow. Those people were the difference makers.

When Clorox bought Deer Park from us after we had bought it from Nestlé, it had two other water companies based in Florida, and eventually my role was to coordinate all three water companies and bring them together as one.

The managers at the water companies owned by Clorox were very different managers and very different people. Once again I was the young marketing guy, and they thought marketing wasn't worth its salt, and they questioned my knowledge on running routes. They had more routes than we had, and just getting these industry old-timers to buy into what I wanted to do was a huge challenge.

But to me, if you're following the same path as everybody else, you're not going to be better than the competition. To be better, you have to try out different things. But we weren't always on the same page, so the consolidation wasn't easy.

We had to make a lot of decisions about who should get what jobs. In one case the founder had a son who was a very competent guy. We tried to get the son to stay, and he stayed for a while, but then he left, and that was a bad outcome for us, because we didn't have a backup internally. We had to go outside.

In the other case it was a smaller company, and the former owner did not have a strong number two, but he needed to be moved out of the day-to-day in that business. Again we needed to search.

In both cases the process took longer because of our cultural differences. The people I wanted—people with a marketing background—didn't mesh with what the other companies were looking for. They wanted leaders with a sales background. They didn't believe market-ing worked, but I knew it had with Deer Park.

While with Nestlé, we took Deer Park from $5 million to $8 million; then as a private company we took it to $12 million. Then when we merged we were doing more expansion to new locations as well as merging these two other companies, so when we were done, ten years later, it was a $65 million company.

Eventually I got the right people in place, and while there was definitely organic growth, having the right leaders working with me was a big reason for the success. The people put in positions of lead-ership create the success.

In this case, because there was a lot of resistance the growth took longer. We eventually did it, and there was a great satisfaction to making it all work. By the time I moved on to McKesson I was ready for greater challenges. You can't compare it to a champion-ship, because the business world isn't a competition where one team is crowned. But my time at Deer Park was definitely a victory.

Leaving is always difficult, but feeling the job is done makes it easier. I appreciate the leaders who spend a lifetime at a company and help it continue to grow over the course of their careers. But that's not for everyone. In this case I knew there were other chal-lenges to tackle, so I happily left with a sense of accomplishment.

BYRON: THE FAREWELL TOUR

A month or so into the 2015–16 season Kobe Bryant announced that he was ending his twenty-year career and retiring from the NBA at the end of the season. It changed the dynamic of the season for me as a coach, and it also changed management's plans for the future of the Lakers.

Just as I tell my players not to think too far ahead and not to play for that next contract, I too wanted to stay focused on winning that season, not thinking about what the team would have to do without Kobe Bryant. He'd been a Laker since my final year as an NBA player in the 1996–97 season.

The season quickly changed course, though, as it became more a farewell tour for Kobe than anything else. Every arena we went to was completely sold out. Ticket prices tripled because fans wanted to see Kobe play his last game in their city. He got gifts and tribute videos and standing ovations, and the game itself became the sideshow in a sense.

The irony was that Kobe just wanted to go out there and win games. He wasn't someone who could ever be distracted. As for the rest of us—myself included, from time to time—it was a different story.

It was difficult trying to go out every single night and win. We had so many young players I was trying to develop into winners while all of this was going on. Publicly I was saying my number one job was to develop those players and win ball games, but in my head I was also trying to make sure Kobe played the right number of minutes each night so that his body would hold up and make it to the last game of the season.

He wanted to play every minute of every game possible, but it was on me as coach to sit him when necessary so his legs would still be working for that last game against the Utah Jazz at home on April 13. We wouldn't play Kobe in back-to-back road games unless it was his last time in a particular city. And if his minutes were up, I'd take him out late in the game, even if we had opportunities to win. If he'd played his limit, I couldn't put him back in.

It was a game plan unlike anything I'd ever had to deal with in

New Jersey, New Orleans, or Cleveland, where we'd just been trying to win games. Winning while developing players and managing a legend's time turned the job in LA into a totally different monster. I was going against my normal coaching style to cater to the fans and management and basically everyone but myself, since the losses landed on my shoulders regardless of the circumstances. Wins became hard to come by, which was something we'd expected, but it was still tough to handle.

It was extremely hard to lose games. After losses I'd wake up two or three times during the night wondering what had happened and what I could have done better. The Kobe factor and the rookie play didn't keep me up at night, but the losing did. I'd get up in the morning and push myself to keep managing and keep going forward in my efforts to make sure these guys continued to get better.

I took every loss hard, and I looked around and wasn't sure it was bothering anyone else. That didn't make it easier. I would tell the guys in practice that if it wasn't bothering them as much as it was bothering me, then something was wrong. Losing got in our heads, and it led to a seventeen-win season.

CHARLIE: SALE OF THE CENTURY

The departure from McKesson Water was a bit different from my exit from Deer Park. I was older, wiser, and probably a bit run down. The stress of turning a company around and dealing with the ups and downs can get to you. You try your hardest to compartmentalize, but it's not easy. In the end it leads to a roller coaster of emotions.

When we sold McKesson Water to Groupe Danone for $1.1 billion dollars, it was a pretty awesome sale. It was the largest sale ever in the bottled water industry. It was Danone's largest purchase ever.

For the sale I worked with McKesson Co. and we hired a great mergers and acquisitions group from Lehman Brothers that was directly involved in helping to sell the company. Nestlé, which owned Arrowhead and quite a number of other home and office delivery companies in the US at the time, was the logical buyer. It wanted to buy the company and would have had the most synergies, but I was afraid that if we sold to Nestlé most of our employees would lose their jobs because there was a tremendous overlap between our head office in LA and Arrowhead's head office in LA.

Danone had very large water holdings outside the US, with Evian and a whole series of other water brands, and a small home and office business in Latin America and in Canada, and that was it. It wanted to become a much larger player in that home and office business, and we were able to maximize the purchase price because we had developed incredible systems and had access to data in real time. If we bought a direct response advertising spot on a Wednesday, we knew whether that commercial had paid out before the next airing on Thursday. If it didn't work, we could cancel Thursday in time. We knew that quickly how well the advertising was doing.

We had developed enterprise software that gave us user-ready data as we were going out to the field on the second day after we closed the books, which was unheard of. We had spectacular systems. Nestlé wanted those systems. Danone wanted those systems. Danone wanted very desperately to have a foothold in the United States for home and office, and we were the biggest one in the country. It was an ideal way for it to really make a statement. So we were able to get the two companies to compete with each other to buy our business, and we got a price that was terrifically high.

It was a good feeling, especially considering the struggles at the beginning. There was a sense of accomplishment not just for me, but also for the entire team of people within the company who knew they'd contributed to this success. By that point we felt like a family, and there was an emotional tie to the sale of the company that almost everyone felt.

Of course, when you are that emotionally invested the pendulum can swing pretty quickly after the sale. You look at the company as your baby, and when someone else is in control it's easy to let emotions get the best of you when decisions are made that you don't agree with.

Part of the deal with the sale of McKesson Water was that I stay on as CEO for at least six months, along with the rest of my senior staff. During that time the executives at Danone ran the company the way they ran their other businesses. They never asked what we had done to make our business so successful. Instead they folded us into the blueprint that they had for running a water company globally, and it didn't work in the United States. They made a number of poor strategic decisions, and it really bit them badly. Ultimately they lost a lot of money and had to sell the company.

I had to stay six months and at six months and one day I called the CEO of the parent company and told him I was going to leave. He asked why and I told him.

"Because the person who's running your water group is going to kill this business, and I don't want to be part of it."

"Would you stay on as a consultant to help us?" he asked.

"Nobody is listening to me as an employee, so why would you listen to me as a consultant?"

There wasn't much to say after that. I told him I wanted out, and that was the end of it.

I didn't know Byron yet when I left McKesson, but all these years of talking to him about his experiences, and watching what happened with the Lakers, changed my perspective a bit on those final months with the company. When I was in the weeds, I felt a strong tie to McKesson Water, and it hurt to watch changes get made, but the truth was that it wasn't the same company anymore. The water might have had the same label on the bottle, but it wasn't the water company I knew and loved.

The same was true with the Lakers team that Byron was coaching. The jerseys were the same, but the culture had changed. It was a different era. You could see it in that meeting with LaMarcus Aldridge, where Lakers management talked about everything but basketball. That foreshadowed Byron's unfortunate departure, which occurred the following summer.

When Byron was playing, owner Jerry Buss had been all about winning. He did whatever it took to have a winning team. If that meant trading Norm Nixon for Byron, he was ready to do it. Back then, when they brought someone in, they sold the winning Lakers culture. Now they were selling Hollywood. In my opinion they'd lost what had made them the great franchise they were in the eighties.

What's great about Byron is that he saw that right away. He was able to compartmentalize and not let his most recent experience with the Lakers sour his great memories and love for the team. I watched him turn the corner and almost immediately move on to his next venture without an ounce of regret or remorse. I wish I had known Byron when I left McKesson, because it took me quite a bit longer to get on his page.

BYRON: OUT WITH A BANG

While it was likely the roughest season of my coaching career, ten years from now the one thing that people will remember most is that seventeenth and final win. No matter where you sat—on the second level of the arena, in the front row next to Jack Nicholson, or at home on a couch somewhere—the last game of the 2015–16 season was a special one for Lakers fans everywhere.

In Kobe Bryant's final NBA game he went out there and left it all on the court. The man played his heart out, turned his game up to a championship level, and gave the fans something they will talk about forever.

As the coach I would just tell the guys to give him the ball. Not just because he was Kobe Bryant and it was his last game, but because he had that Mamba look in his eyes. He had the hot hand, and as I tried to explain to the guys all season, you have to feed the hot hand.

I also had to remind the rest of the team from time to time to keep their spacing and not just stand out there and watch the show, because if they doubled Kobe at any point they needed to be open for a shot. They needed to spread the floor and be ready if the ball came their way. That's always a problem for young guys when there's a figure like Kobe on the team, but in this final game it was even more of an issue because it was a spectacular game to watch.

Through it all I don't think I drew up one play. During time-outs I would name the play we were running and remind Kobe where he'd be catching the ball. It was really that simple. Once he got it going it was just "Get him the ball." It took them eighty-two games to do it, but our young guys realized he had the hot hand.

I guess that's something I can take away from that experience with the Lakers. Those guys grew up a lot over the two seasons and I think they'll be better for it down the road. Kobe's last game was also Gary Vitti's last game with the organization, and as it turned out it was my last game too.

The two years didn't go how I'd wanted them to, and I didn't get another year to see what I could do with the team. That's just the way it goes sometimes. Charlie thought I got a raw deal. I think he was angrier than I was when he found out they'd called me in on a Sunday night to tell me it was over. Earlier in the week I had been with Mitch Kupchak and Jim Buss at a meeting at UCLA, discussing a partnership with the school's medical staff, and by Sunday my time with the team was over. Clearly they'd known I was on my way out, but they hadn't felt the need to be up front about it. That was the new culture in the Lakers organization, and Charlie was quick to point that out to me. Even if they had kept me on, similar issues would have continued to arise throughout my time there.

Being around Charlie and seeing how he conducts business is a reminder that there are people out there leading the right way. As an honest leader, Charlie was angry when he heard the news. I could see that vein in his head pop out when he would talk about it, which actually made me smile a bit. I have the same passion for my job, but I have no hard feelings, and in the end coaching the Lakers was still a dream come true even if at times the job was a nightmare.

At least the two-year run had a magical ending, with a final game by Kobe that I was happily the head coach for. He finished the night with sixty points (the most of any player in that season), including thirteen unanswered points in the fourth quarter, to give us the victory when we had been down by ten points. During time-outs he was breathing heavily and I could see on his face that he was giving it everything he had. It was pure adrenaline keeping him going at the end.

At one point I was worried that it was too much. I didn't need him falling over in his final game, but I knew his mentality was that he had the rest of his life to rest, so he wanted to be out there.

What makes him a winner isn't the sixty points. It isn't the thirteen unanswered. It isn't the nineteen thousand fans in the arena who went nuts with every shot. It wasn't even the 5.2 million who tuned in to watch the game on ESPN2 (since the Golden State Warriors were going for a record of their own on ESPN).

The number that makes Kobe a legend is the number seventeen. That win—in a season when wins were hard to come by—was the only thing that mattered. He didn't score sixty because he wanted to score sixty. That's what he needed to score for the team to win the game.

From day one when he entered the league and wasn't even a starter, all that mattered to Kobe was getting the win. Now at his last game it was still the only thing that mattered. That's why he's a future Hall of Famer, and I'm glad the other guys on the team were watching.

CHARLIE: CLEAR THE MIND

The day I announced that I was leaving Groupe Danone, Ric Kayne called me and wanted to have lunch to get me involved with Glacier Water Vending. He was the primary owner of Glacier Water Vending at the time, and he called me every day for nearly a year to get me involved.

On that first day I was honest with him and told him I didn't want to do anything. I had gone through a very stressful period for ten years at McKesson Water, and when I left I was really burned out.

My time at McKesson was mostly positive. By the end I didn't just have the respect of the employees, there was actual love there. I got cards and letters and well wishes from many—a far cry from the hate mail early on—and most were genuinely sad to see me go.

I felt the same way. They were all such a big part of my life. The company was a big part of my life, maybe too big.

For a long time after I left I was holding on to an annoyance about what the acquirer of our business was doing to the company, and a lot of the senior managers who remained were calling me and complaining about what had happened since I left. I was carrying it for longer than I would've liked.

I needed a true sabbatical after leaving to really clear my head, remove business thoughts from my mind, and breathe a little before making decisions about my future.

I got a number of proposals to do consulting, and people were throwing ridiculously high dollar figures at me, and I just didn't want to do anything. I just wanted to chill out. It really was important to just get my balance, and during that period, Peggy and I set up a donor-advised trust with the California Community Foundation, and we started to get much more involved in philanthropy.

I was looking to balance my life more by giving back to the community while I was also gainfully employed. I taught a seminar on corporate communication from the CEO perspective at the Annenberg School for Communication and Journalism at the University of Southern California. I got involved with the USC Wrigley Institute for Environmental Studies. And we started to look for charities that Peggy and I, as well as our children, Emi and Mike, were passionate about.

We found organizations that we could contribute to financially and in other ways. I was hardly doing nothing during my time off, but I was able to stay away from worrying about quarterly earnings statements, employee problems, and everything that had really been occupying my time for over thirty years.

Once I was truly released from that world I was able to focus on what I wanted to do in this next stage of my career. Ultimately I decided I did not want to work full time, because I wanted to spend more time on philanthropic areas, travel, and other things that gave me more fulfillment.

When you are between jobs or looking to make a major change, you have to ask yourself, "Is the skill set that I possess today good enough for me to continue to be competitive in the marketplace in my area? If not, what education do I need?" The process of looking for a new job is a full-time job in itself, so you should lay out your plan in the same way you would lay out a business plan for running a company.

I was fortunate enough that I didn't have to work. So for me it was more about finding balance. That took me the better part of a year, and when I'd done it I called Ric and began investing in Glacier and many other companies. I took my skill set to the boardroom and built a portfolio of companies where I invested and held a board seat, including Freshpet, which excites me as much as any company that I have worked with throughout my career.

X's and O's

- Everyone on the team plays a role in success, and the resources you need are all around you.

- The longer you wait to put the right team together, the longer it will take to find success.

- If the culture is changing for the worse and you can't affect the outcome, then it's time to move on.

- Take time to clear your mind before creating a new plan.

Chapter 20

Beyond the Boards

"Don't ever put yourself in the position to wish you could hop in a time machine." —*Ray Allen*

Being a leader is a 24-7 job, and educational opportunities to improve as a leader are everywhere. Learn from your friends and family and sometimes even complete strangers, and you'll find new opportunities at every turn.

BYRON: OUTSIDE PERSPECTIVE

The further removed I was from my playing days the more the game seemed to change. It's not just the style of play, but also the business end of the NBA and the personalities of the players. If I was going to be successful, I had to grow with the game. I had to constantly change my approach, but more importantly, I had to continue to understand people. I had to talk to players and owners and do what I could to figure out how their minds worked.

The best way to do that was to continue adding new perspective to the way I looked at life and coaching. Meeting Charlie was an eye-opener. I discovered early on how much we had in common, but I also realized that the differences between our backgrounds and experiences could help continue to mold me as a leader.

No matter how old you are or how long you've been in the game, you're always learning, and Charlie helped change everything from the way I eat and drink to the way I coach.

As our relationship blossomed, we decided to take a trip to Boston so I could see where Charlie grew up. He introduced me to a lot of his Boston friends and they took us around the city—a city I used to despise.

Boston was the Lakers' biggest rival during my playing days, and the dislike for the Celtics carried itself over into a dislike for the city. The fans hated us, the weather was terrible, and it was usually a place I couldn't wait to leave.

When I went back with Charlie, Boston was a completely different city to me. We walked the Freedom Trail, saw Faneuil Hall and Old North Church, visited the cemetery where Paul Revere was buried, and really soaked in the history of the city and the history of the United States. As it turns out, Boston is beautiful. I even went to three Red Sox–Yankees games and proudly rooted for the Yankees without making one enemy the entire game—even though the Yankees won all three.

On the trip I made a few friends from among Charlie's childhood buddies. Later in the year they all went to Las Vegas, and I met up with them for part of the trip. You never know where you can make a new friend, but it wasn't just about camaraderie. That trip to Boston completely changed my perspective on the city. In all my years in the NBA, I never got out from under being a player who would show up for a dogfight against Larry Bird and Kevin McHale. I never saw the real Boston.

It used to be one of my least favorite cities in the country, and now I think it's probably one of my favorites. If I can change my perspective on a city that I hated, I can change my perspective on anything. That's a difference Charlie made in my life.

No matter what age you are, there is always room to grow. The worst thing you can do as a leader is be so set in your ways that you refuse to try new things. Before I met Charlie I used to eat steak medium well. That's just how I grew up eating it. He went on and on about how it loses the flavor that way and, as it turned out, he was right. Now I eat steak medium rare.

That open-mindedness carries over. This generation of player is totally different from the generation I'm used to, so every day is still a learning process for me, because as the leader I need to continue to learn what makes the new guys tick. I want to be able to speak their language, and that happens when I listen, not just to them, but also to everyone around them and everyone in their age bracket. Spending time with Charlie is a constant reminder that the first step to speaking someone's language is being willing to listen.

CHARLIE: PRIDE IS CONTAGIOUS

During that trip to Boston I also took Byron to the suburb where I grew up and showed him my old home and some of the places I would go as a child. I think the whole experience helped change his view not only of the city, but also of the core of who I am.

You can meet people and learn new things from them every day in life, but really getting to know them adds even more layers of learning potential. I try to educate myself in a number of ways, but I haven't learned as much from any other method as I have from asking people for their insight. I've done it at the office my entire career.

I'll let people know that I don't know everything all the time, which helps me and serves a dual purpose, as most people genuinely enjoy when their boss asks for their advice.

Gaining knowledge from people outside the office is even better. I enjoy being around people. Everyone you meet has a story, and there's no person who isn't interesting. You just have to get them to want to share their story with you. Unlocking that safe brings pearls of wisdom.

You have to be willing to get brushed aside because some people won't trust you or won't want to share, but when it does work—which is most of the time—you'll leave the conversation a better person.

I've met people on airplanes and in museums and restaurants who have touched my life in some way, but with Byron I think we both felt we had more to offer each other than a surface-level relationship.

Just as he'd come to Boston, I went to see where Byron spent his formative years in Inglewood. He showed me the home he grew up in—a very modest home but obviously very well kept—and the playground where he played basketball with his friends. He took me to the local soul food restaurant and the Costco, and in both places the employees were the children of people Byron had grown up with. Byron was still a hero to them, both for his success and for never leaving the neighborhood. He never outgrew his roots. It is the foundation of his personality.

He still has the same half-dozen friends from elementary school, and I know all of them now and they're all great guys. These are guys who protected him so he wouldn't get into trouble. To this day they treat him the same way they treated him when he was ten or twelve years old. Every one of them has had a very successful career. None of them were beaten down by the environment. In most cases they had parents who pushed them to see beyond the neighborhood. One was kicked out of his house, and Byron's mother took him in. He lived with the Scotts for six months, and he'll never forget how much Byron's parents meant to him. At Byron's mother's funeral this particular friend gave a moving speech about how much Byron's parents helped shape his life.

What I loved the most was the pride that Byron had in the neighborhood. You could see it in his face and hear it in his words when he talked about Inglewood. You read about the gangs and other difficulties in communities like Inglewood, but that's not the real story. They are proud people raising their kids the same way I was raised by my parents. His friends all had core family values and a strong work ethic. It isn't where you live that defines a person; it's how you live.

The pride Byron has in his hometown is the same pride he has in the Lakers, and the same pride he takes in every job he does. It's inspirational to watch and it's a daily reminder that you need that level of pride to be a strong leader.

That pride is now helping both of us on the business front. Byron has come to bank meetings and done work with Freshpet, a company he's now an investor in. Where he's been the most helpful is in being available to meet people who are important to the company. People don't always want to hear me talk, so bringing in a fresh face like Byron can really make a difference. He knows about the company and can talk about the business, but most importantly he gives the people we are doing business with the sense that there is more to the company than they realized.

The involvement of someone like Byron, who is so successful in another field, is intriguing to potential partners, and it's helped us with our sales programs a great deal. Obviously everyone wants to talk about basketball if they see Byron, but it always comes back to his relationship with Freshpet. He can say, "I'm an investor in the company, I know senior management, and I learn more and more about what they're doing and I'm really impressed. I've been a dog owner and I see what the products are and how our dogs have reacted to it." He knows where the company is headed. He doesn't have to get into a great level of detail, but his involvement and his support have huge benefits for us.

BYRON: OUTSIDE THE BUBBLE

Expanding my horizons into Charlie's world has been good for me as a person and has helped me become a more well-rounded coach and leader. Most people think they are defined by the job they have, but I don't think that's true. Yes, I was a Laker, but there's more to me than that. Being successful in business ventures or in broadcasting is just as important, and when I do return to coaching, I'll have even more knowledge to bring to the court.

Getting out there into the world isn't just something I needed to do for myself; it's something I needed to do with the team from time to time as well. Often in the grind of the long season the guys get lost in their bubble. They get so into their routine of working out, practicing, playing games, eating, and sleeping that they forget there's a whole world out there. It becomes draining, and at times it affects their ability to win.

On the plane or away from the game I try to talk to guys, hear about their lives outside basketball, and get to know them as people instead of just ballplayers. The stories you hear sometimes are pretty crazy, but then again it's just a reminder that we are all human beings.

We're going to make mistakes in life, and they may affect our ability to work. We're going to have problems at home or other issues to deal with, and that's going to change our effort level at the office (so to speak).

That's why I've always encouraged players to live their lives—travel, see the world, try new things. I don't want them to waste their time on distractions like partying or useless entertainment. I want them to see how the rest of the world lives and learn a little something.

A lot of these guys know only two ways of life: really poor and really rich. There's a whole world in the middle that they've got to be in touch with if they want to be great. Everyone in every position in life has something to offer, and once you realize that, you find learning opportunities everywhere.

It's the same thing on the court. Positions don't even matter anymore. All that matters is whether you can play basketball. The position is just a title. I like to put five guys out there who can just flat-out play, who know how to play together and are very intelligent. I don't necessarily worry about positions. You see that with successful teams like Golden State, where everyone from the two to five positions is basically the same height. They're versatile enough to do that.

That's how life is. Positions don't matter. Anyone can be a leader. Anyone can be a teacher. When you step outside your bubble, you start to see that.

You can take your knowledge and apply it to anything, which is one of the reasons I invited Charlie to the Lakers facility to sit in on some film sessions with the players and speak at one of the coaches' meetings. His view on leadership was an asset to my team of coaches, who were struggling to stay motivated during these losing seasons. He stood up there and told them that a great leader isn't just someone who is leading when things are going well, but also someone who has the ability to continue to push people to improve and pave the way for future success. He looked them in the eyes and told them he was proud of their leadership skills and the progress we'd made during that trying previous season in which we'd won seventeen games, and it made a huge impact on them.

The players and coaches heard my voice every day. They listened and strove for greatness. But hearing a different voice talk about leadership changed their perspective and kept the fire burning for success. Even though Charlie never played organized basketball, they hung on every word he said and believed in his message. Sometimes when people don't have time to step outside their bubble, a leader can come in and motivate them. Charlie showed up and did just that.

CHARLIE: CHANGE YOUR BODY, CHANGE YOUR MIND

There is a Buddhist philosophy of never having a clenched fist. The logic is that if your fist is clenched, you're never going to be able to grab something else. If you have an open hand, yes, what you have in your hand may fly off, but you don't know what's going to come and land on your hand. And I think that in life it's very important to be open. Part of that is being willing to share what you can with other people. When you do that, you'll find that most of the time they'll offer something to you in return.

I was happy to lend whatever knowledge I could to Byron and his team of coaches, and frankly I was honored that he asked. From the moment Byron and I met, he's been a wealth of knowledge to me, and it started in the gym.

When I lived in Switzerland I was overeating and drinking too much Swiss wine and I put on a fair amount of weight. I looked at myself in the mirror and wasn't happy. So when I was there I started running and did pull-ups and push-ups at different stations around the park. When I moved to New York I ran in Central Park and started running races—working my way up to running the New York City Marathon twice.

During those years my workout was almost all running. I didn't belong to a gym, I did no weight lifting at all, and I didn't even stretch very much. I'd just go to Central Park and run. When I moved out to LA I started to have some knee problems. Driving from West LA to Pasadena, which is potentially an hour each way, was rough on my knees. I'd get out of that car in pain. That's when I decided to join Equinox and run on a treadmill instead of pounding the concrete.

By the time I met Byron I was working out six days a week, doing either an hour on the elliptical or an hour on the treadmill without ever changing the resistance. I added five hundred crunches in various forms to the mix and thought I was getting a great workout. After we became friendly, Byron said, "You know, you're not really benefiting as much as you could from the way you're doing your cardio. Working shorter periods while constantly increasing the resistance is going to be much more beneficial than staying on a machine for an hour."

One of us suggested that we give this workout thing a try together and the rest is history. We went up from one machine a day to six different machines, and turned what had been an hour-long workout into a three-hour workout. I was really working my body to the limit, and I started losing weight.

Then he said, "If you really want to get in shape, you've got to add weights." It was the same message that Gary Vitti had passed on to him decades before, but that bit of knowledge still held true.

We started working all the major body parts, doing crunches in between the various exercises and continuing with the cardio machines. We also went outside once a week and ran the outdoor track and the stands at UCLA, ran around the perimeter of the campus, or hiked in the Santa Monica Mountains. This was all going on six days a week.

The lifting was new to me, and the cardio and the crunches were more than he was used to as well, but we pushed each other and competed, and to this day we enjoy every second of it. I'm seventy now, and he and I have been doing this since I was sixty, and according to my general physician I'm in much better overall health today than I was ten years ago.

Something like adding weights to your workout may seem simple, but that advice changed Byron's life in the eighties and it's changed mine over the past ten years. You can't underestimate knowledge or make assumptions about where you can and cannot learn new things. We were both in the gym one day and managed to change each other's lives forever.

BYRON: PAY IT FORWARD

It's true. If it weren't for those workouts, this relationship wouldn't be what it is today, and that friendship is changing many lives. Whenever the Lakers were at home I'd bring Charlie to the Lakers facility to work out. The guys would see this older gentleman working hard at the crack of dawn and realize they needed to step up their game. It sent a subtle message that we don't tolerate slackers on this team. I think it helped.

Charlie also helped me with my basketball camp. He does a good deal of charity work, much of which involves youth at risk and job creation. When he was at McKesson, it had a foundation, and youth at risk were one of their key areas of interest. He saw a lot of organizations that were dealing with teenagers and providing after-school programs to keep kids off the street.

Because of his experience, he suggested that we add life skills training to my basketball camp. At a previous camp Charlie had introduced a system that included four hours of basketball and four hours of life skills training a week, and if a teenager completed the ten weeks he or she was guaranteed one hundred hours of paid internship at a local company. He tracked how they did in school, and everyone who was in the program improved their grades.

Life skills training really goes hand in hand with making leaders of these kids, so it was a great addition to our camp. In the first year we brought in guest speakers, but the plan is to make this training more of a core component.

So simple things can really change lives. Whether it's in the gym or out in the real world, we enhanced each other's lives, and now we get to pass it on to benefit the lives of others. The only way to make that happen is to constantly educate yourself and spend every minute striving for greatness.

CHARLIE: EVERYDAY RISK

There is risk involved in relationship building. Men, especially, want to maintain the veneer of macho and cool. Especially as you get older, it's rare that you'll develop a friendship where you let down your guard and really get into who you are and what you believe in. You're never going to develop a truly meaningful friendship if you're not willing to take risks and step out of your comfort zone. You won't develop the kind of lifetime relationships that have deep meaning if you're not willing to open up about who you are, what your fears are, and where your comfort is. Plus if you can't step out of your comfort zone at a place like the gym, you probably can't do it at work either.

You want friends who challenge you and push you to be better. You want them to be receptive to the same from you. What really impressed me about Byron was his willingness to try new things. He's wonderfully open to new ideas and new ways of thinking. He's very analytical and very bright, but his universe was somewhat limited by the career he's had. But he's willing to step outside that, and that to me is wonderful.

We also push each other to stay competitive, both inside the gym and out. When you're a CEO or a coach of a sports team there is competition all around you, but a real leader likes to win at everything. So we compete.

Byron and I play five hundred rummy, backgammon, and various other games, and there's always a bet. The bet is always ridiculously small. We could be on a plane together for five hours from LA to New York and we'll spend the whole time playing cards. If one person wins or loses five dollars in five hours it's a catastrophe. We're playing for pennies, but we're really playing for bragging rights, which are so much more valuable than anything else.

For the wagers we made a "B&C jar," and however much money one of us loses in the game, he has to put a matching amount in the jar. So we're doubling our losses. Whoever wins gets to keep the jar at his home. When Byron is winning he keeps it in his car, and he takes every opportunity to lord it over me that he is the holder of the jar.

Everything we do is important to us and has significance. From work to the gym to these two- and three-dollar card games, we take pride in what we do. We care, and whether we are a team or battling each other for the B&C jar, we always want to win.

By opening up and getting to know each other we've managed to keep our minds, bodies, and competitive edge sharp. Byron and I were two people who on paper seemed like total opposites, but we gave each other a chance, saw that we could learn a lot from each other, and accomplished a lot of great things together. Leaders make it happen. It seemed impossible to the other people in the gym, and to this day people ask us about it. But we formed a lifelong partnership and made each other stronger leaders. If we can do it, so can you. It's worth the risk.

X's and O's

- Sometimes the least likely person will impact your life the most.

- Seeing something from a new perspective will open your mind to new ways to succeed.

- Expand your horizons, but never forget where you came from.

- Take winning seriously, but have fun while doing it.

Acknowledgments

For years people told us that we should write a book, which was a nice thought in between sets at the gym. When we sat down to actually do it, we realized writing a book isn't so easy. With any task in business, sports, or life, it takes a team to achieve success, and we wouldn't be here today with a product we are extremely proud of without the help of many great people.

Linda Rush, Dennis Blue, Kathleen Torrell, Bob Gura, Bob Bolingbroke, Dick Kassar, Scott Morris, David Basto, Brian McInerney, Bill Armstrong, David Shladovsky, Bob Iritani, Larry Lewis, Paul Pressey, Gary Vitti, Kobe Bryant, Larry Brown, Derek McGee, Marilyn Tang, and Chris Paul all took time out of their busy days to help us remember a few key life moments and also to make sure that our facts were correct. Also, James Cox and Nina Moore gave early encouragement to our book efforts.

A special thanks to Byron's dad, Robert Marsh, who not only walked us through Byron's childhood for this book but paved the way for its success by raising Byron into the leader he is today.

Charlie's family—Peggy, Emi, and Michael Norris—were helpful throughout the entire book-writing process (and every day of Charlie's life). Michael deserves a special thank-you for helping to shape the direction of the book during its early stages. Friends

Charlotte Jacobs, Lena Goldberg, and Pete Chiarelli read several drafts of the book.

Early supporters who helped get this creation off the ground include Todd Smith, who became our manager; Howard Hart, our attorney; and David Vigliano, our literary agent, who introduced us to our wonderful editor, Kate Hartson, executive editor of Center Street Books.

Along with Kate, the entire team at Center Street was by our side at every step in the editing, marketing, and production process leading to our book launch. Lending their expertise and guiding us to the finish line were Rolf Zettersten, publisher; Patsy Jones, VP, marketing and publicity; Laini Brown, senior publicist; Billy Clark, VP of sales; Gina Wynn, sales director, and the entire sales team; Andrea Glickson, marketing director; Anthony Goff, publisher of Hachette Audio; Sara Beth Haring, marketing assistant; and Grace Tweedy Johnson, editorial assistant.

We'd also like to thank our writer, Jon Warech, who understood our vision and voices and brought them to life. He would also like to thank the team at Hachette and Kirby Kim, Joy Warech, Zoë Levy, Erin and Brad Fox, Mikey Glazer, Melissa Rappaport, Robert Eth, and Jessica Contrastano.

Finally, we'd like to thank Earvin Johnson for not only lending his Magic touch to this book, but supporting us every single step of the way. Just like on the basketball court, with his assist we were able to really make this book a slam-dunk success.